Max & Carol —

Finally!

Best,
Chandler Smith

and Man Created God...

and Man Created God...

Chandler Smith

VISION BOOKS INTERNATIONAL
MILL VALLEY, CALIFORNIA

Copyright 2000 © Chandler Smith

All rights reserved. No part of this book may be reproduced in any form or by any electronic or mechanical means, including information storage and retrieval systems, without written pernission from the publisher.

Library of Congress Number: 00 132981

ISBN: 1-56550-086-5

Book design: Robert Brekke
Publishers Design Group

Vision Books International
415.451.7188

Printed in the United States

ACKNOWLEDGMENTS

THE WRITING OF THIS BOOK is due in large measure to the contributions of three special women. The first is my wife, Dorothy, whose text suggestions and skilled, indefatigable proof reading are more than appreciated. The second is Jan Tourte, my computer expert, without whom I would have been stuck in cyberspace. The third is Sharon Jones, who guided these writings to publication. To all I extend a special thank you and send a flower.

CONTENTS

Introduction

PART ONE

Questioning Christianity   3
Creationism   8
Evolution   12
Molecular Evolution   39

PART TWO

The Good, the Misleading, & the Doubtful   47
Atheism   58
Alternative Beliefs   67
The Choice   79

PART THREE

Church-State Separation   93
Abortion   105
Homosexuality, HIV, and AIDS   114
Controlling Crime   120
The Impossibility of Peace   130
Spectral Examples   141
Deterrence   151
The Dominion of Fear   158

Conclusion

Introduction

The purpose of this book is to examine the advantages of Secular Humanism over the beliefs of various religions, especially Christianity, with its sizable following that suspends reality in favor of faith. The intention is to embrace a belief that does not depend on the emotion of faith in something ethereal, but instead is anchored in man's own self-reliance. This requires a consideration of certain religious ideas, and a review of the purveyors of these ideas. Moreover, it is necessary to consider the nature of creationism and compare it with that of evolution. The brutal, but probably true, fact is that we humans are alone on the crust of this minor planet, and that it is up to us, by ourselves, to solve the problems of our own existence. The belief that accommodates this concept is Secular Humanism. First formally recognized in 1933, it has the courage to face reality without leaning on fanciful thoughts unsupported by objective evidence.

While turning away from a deity-centered belief, it is important to retain the moral foundations of most religions; for without morality, there is no discipline to behavior; and, without discipline, behavior turns to savagery. Therefore, humanity cannot be civilized without morality. For this reason, Christ's truly moral teachings are central to the success of any enterprise, and on that account, must be preserved, not because of a belief in his divinity, but because of his universal message. Truth and justice and compassion are necessary to the human condition. Society without morality is unthinkable.

Does Secular Humanism provide advantages over conventional Christianity? Yes, and in five different ways. The first is that Christianity encourages the merging of church and state for political gain; whereas, Humanism disallows the merger. The second is that Christianity preaches forgiveness, and then allows stiff punishment for most criminals; whereas, Humanism recommends the abolition of punishment for certain crimes. The third is that Christianity accepts just wars; whereas, Humanism recommends the abolition of war through nonviolence. It also eliminates religious differences which have a war-causing effect. Fourth, Christianity seems unable to solve the very important questions of contraceptives and abortion in a manner acceptable to both sides; whereas, Humanism suggests a new orientation to the problem. And finally, Humanism accepts homosexuality as a legitimate lifestyle; whereas Christianity tends to reject that practice to the point of stepping on Constitutional rights.

These are weighty matters, and are presented in Part III, which consists of eight essays that deal with controversial and emotional issues. It should be understood that the author is not authorized to speak for the Secular Humanist organization. He speaks for himself, although he supports the Humanists' concepts.

The truth must always be expressed. It doesn't matter the consequences. It doesn't matter the disruption or the convictions that are overturned. It doesn't matter that the discoverer is maligned. It only matters that the discovery is valid. All human belief and all human activity should be regulated and disciplined by the truth.

It was Darwin, especially, who brought the importance of objective evidence to the public when he published his book on the origin of species in 1859. That book set before the public the grand question of whether the scientific concept of evolution should or should not prevail over the religious concept of creationism. It was the mass of evidence, as will be reviewed in this book, as well as the continuing accumulation of evidence, that settled the question in favor of evolution.

Since the time of Darwin, other examples of progress based on objective evidence have included the acceptance of relativity, the nature of radiation, control of the human genome, our understanding of quantum mechanics, the unending expansion of the universe, organ transplantation, and the cloning of mammals. From all of this comes the conclusion that objective evidence is the requirement of progress.

No objective evidence supports the idea that Christ was divine or that God exists. Without such evidence, religions are based solely on unfounded speculations. So, while science advances on the firm ground of evidence, religions are left treading water in the endless mire of faith. That is the dilemma.

If two items of faith, the divinity of Christ and the existence of God, are in fact unfounded speculation, what would it mean? It would mean that there is no supernatural Being, no heaven or hell, no resurrection, and no miracles. It would mean that man would have to take charge of his own destiny. He would have to manage his own affairs, and mismanagement would have its costs.

It is we who cut down the rain forests, glorify the machinery of war, destroy the ozone shield, tolerate the rising global temperature, poison the forests with acid rain, overlook the co-existence of embarrassing wealth with grinding poverty, brazenly prepare for the moral obscenity of nuclear war, disregard the control of populations, and turn away from the indelible stain of racial inequities. These matters lie at our doorstep, and it is we who must take responsibility for them. These problems are not attributable to God, but to those in power who fail to do something about them – namely, us.

At this moment , as we sit here in our comfortable repose, the world builds its bombs, prepares for war, and blithely overlooks the radioactive poisons that float down on the wind. We now kill those who commit the crime of murder, as if evil can abolish evil. We shame ourselves for treating fellow humans in this way. Yet we go along with pious quotes from the Bible in justifying popular public policy issues. So, voices must be raised. The truth must be known. It is only we who control our own destiny. We have no higher calling than to take care of each other. That is the message of this book.

• • • • •

PART ONE

THREE FACTORS VALIDATE the question of whether God exists. The first is that a claim without evidence is meaningless; the second is that only objective evidence is reliable; and, the third is that what does not exist produces no evidence. Analysis of these factors reveals that no credible evidence supports the existence of God. Therefore, it is my intuition that the concept of God is a myth. An explanation of the analysis is given within. There is also a nod to creationism, and a review of evolution. The latter suggests that God may not be needed to keep society civilized, a main theme of organized religion.

◆ ◆ ◆ ◆ ◆

1

*The presence of God is
as imperceptible as the
absence of God.*

Questioning Christianity

FOR THE PAST 2,000 YEARS, Western culture has found its moral strength in Christianity. The fundamental pillars of Christianity are the beliefs that Christ is divine, and that God exists. Neither of these is seriously challenged, and ministries the world over proclaim them as true. It would appear blasphemous to question either belief, but it is necessary when it is noticed that there is no factual justification for presuming either the existence of God or the divinity of Christ.

Subjective evidence comes from the mind and is unaffected by the external world. One might believe that the color yellow is more beautiful than any other color. While that might be someone's sincere belief, it could not be proven. It's a personal or subjective point of view. Or, one might believe a deceased friend has called from heaven. That couldn't be proven either, even though it seems very real to the person feeling the connection. It is subjective.

Objective evidence is different because it can be proved. It's in a form that can be weighed, measured, and expressed in numbers. It's factual. It requires no interpretation. If a melon is said to be heavier than another melon, each can be weighed, and the scale will tell which is the heavier. That result is independent of personal opinion. Moreover, when others weigh the same melons, the results are the same, so the results are independently reproducible. This deals only with material objects, including humans.

However, the definition of objective must also include that which can be observed. Christ existed and preached a message against man's inhumanity to man. There is evidence of this; it was observed and recorded. It is evidence in the matter of Christ's divinity or God's existence that is subjective. It comes from the Bible in terms of stories and opinion. It comes from men who claim to have had words with God, or from those who have attributed favorable circumstances to their belief in the divinity of Christ. There is no physical matter to be measured, there is no scientific observation. The crucifixion of Christ, for example, was observed and is accepted as fact. But the writings of the Disciples are devoid of reproducible fact. They are subjective.

The Bible was not written until many years after Christ died. The authors were many; they came from several different countries; and they were largely unknown. Also, the text has been revised many times. The biblical stories were fabricated by men. They were not only apocryphal, they conflicted with the physical laws of nature. The resurrection and the immaculate conception contradict the physical laws of nature, and are accordingly unreliable.

The Bible is a rich compendium of subjective evidence. Many of the stories were written for teaching purposes, to guide people, but it was guidance based on the Disciples' interpretations of Christ's teachings, lessons which included their individual, subjective biases.

A large segment of the Christian faith, Roman Catholics, believe in the infallibility of a man who allows himself to be called the Holy Father, and the Protestants have a version of this with their Archbishop of Canterbury. For this reason, it takes nerve to stand up in public and even suggest, let alone declare, that all of this is based on unreliable speculation. It can not be done without being utterly convinced that the Christian faith is not valid, and that there is something better to take its place.

There are also the directions of the clergy to the faithful who are governed by their instructions to be considered. Millions upon millions of lives are affected by the clerical directions, from how to behave in daily matters to how to anticipate the presumed afterlife. Also, the public belief is a massive conviction; it won't be easily moved because there is comfort in thinking that there is a God who cares for all persons. Most would find it troubling to dwell upon this subject.

People would have to admit that they are worshipping a formulation made by man. Now, if they want to worship such a formulation, that is their business, but as truth requires, they must be willing to admit that their belief originated with man, contradicts the physical laws of nature, and is without the support of credible evidence. There are those, and their number is legion, who don't give a whit about logic or evidence, or the laws of nature. They want to cling to their beliefs that Christ was divine and that God exists, regardless of all else. It gives them external meaning, even if these beliefs seems about as sensible as that of the Tarahumara Indians in Mexico who worship the moon. Because both are without evidence, the two belief systems are of equal merit.

It may be asked whether anyone benefits from denying the divinity of Christ or the existence of God. If we let Christ be divine, and if we let God exist, then we not only live an illusion, we teach it to our children. We teach them to believe that an illusion is truth. We have to accept that those who believe in God do so because they want to believe in him, and they should accept that fact, also. Many believe in Christ because they have accepted him as divine. The definition of a divine person is one who can suspend the laws of nature, and, therefore, perform miracles. The facts of his legacy are strong enough; he does not need divinity to merit allegiance.

That's the pity of it; there is so much to teach. Christ's message is as valid now as it was 2,000 years ago. His teachings have value for all peoples, regardless of age. They should be taught on the basis of utility, rather than on the basis of the myth of divinity, and not on the hope of a celestial guru who rewards the good, punishes the evil, and ordains the future. Prayers to such a myth are not likely to be fruitful.

There are those who would worry that without a system of believing in God, without an accountability to his plan, humans would have no reason to behave morally, would have no higher power to be superior to power on earth. The response is that humans know right from wrong and should be lead by their appreciation and understanding of what they know to be true for a just life.

We have had those who have used their talents and professions to teach of the strength and fragility of the earth, to inspire all to know of the beauty and importance of its peoples, plants, animals, and sea life and their interdependence with each other and with the geographical and atmospheric features of this earth. We are not children, and should not be unduly impressed by the elaborate vestments of the clergy, nor by the solemn call to prayers, nor by soaring cathedrals, magnificent as they are, nor by the liturgical presumption that a man can suspend the laws of nature. None of this will help us in the trials ahead.

It is time to turn back to reality. The direction of that turn is best rooted in the moral messages of Jesus and like prophets. If we, as a species, are to survive, it will be by recognizing the need for morality, and abiding by its injunctions. Jesus is still to be glorified because it was his message. Religion should not be the worship of the supernatural; it should be the worship of a moral code and fidelity to it. The objective words of prophets, philosophers, scientists, humanitarians, educators, writers and those who speak out for reasonableness, who denounce hatred, and who remind us that we are all one on the earth and do not need a supernatural element to make the messages true, are to live by.

• • • • •

2

Was it all created in six days?

Creationism

CREATIONISM IS IMPORTANT in a general discussion of religion. It's a fundamentalist postulate that the world and all the various forms of life were created by God out of nothing.[1] A fundamentalist can be defined as a person who believes in the literal word of the Bible. The whole achievement of creation was completed in six days according to the Bible.[2] It's in Genesis, the first Book of the New Testament.

But in 1831, an English naturalist named Charles Darwin embarked on a round the world trip on a ship named the Beagle. He took copious travel notes, collected many specimens, and after arriving home, gradually formulated a theory called evolution. This theory was described in a book, *On the Origin of Species by Natural Selection*, which was published in England in 1859. The theory was that all living things originated independently of the biblical account of creationism. It was based on the specimens and observations that Darwin made on his long sea voyage. It was thus objective and scientific. By 1880, evolution was almost unanimously accepted by the American scientific community.[3] That set up a huge controversy between the Christians who believed in the biblical account of the beginning, and the scientists who believed in Darwin's account of the beginning. It was the Christians versus the scientists. The dispute was ongoing, and even today there are proponents for both sides. So in order to understand these two divergent points of view, we should begin with a brief account of creationism.

William Jennings Bryan, who ran twice for the presidency of the United States, was a Christian fundamentalist. He believed that the cause of World War I was due, in part, to the theory of evolution, which substituted the law of the jungle for the law of Jesus Christ. He also thought that the theory of evolution would interfere with the faith of children in the Bible. Therefore, in the 1920s a crusade was launched to ban the teaching of evolution in the public schools, and by 1930, several states had passed such a law.[4]

Some creationists claimed scientific credentials. One was Harry Rimmer, a Presbyterian minister and self-styled research scientist, who believed that Genesis described two creations, one beginning millions of years ago, and the other occurring 6,000 years ago and taking just six days. Another creationist was George Price, a Seven Day Adventist who had taught himself geology. He believed all life was created 6,000 years ago and that a universal flood at the time of Noah explained the fossil record on which the theory of evolution was partly based. A third interpretation of Genesis was by W.J. Bryan who thought the six days of creation were actually longer periods than 24 hours each. The creationists couldn't reach agreement on the interpretation of Genesis.[5]

The controversy between fundamentalists and scientists came to a head in 1925, when John Scopes, a high school teacher, was tried for teaching evolution in a public school. The trial was in Tennessee, a state that had declared such teaching to be unlawful. The trial emphasized the scarcity of distinguished scientists in the creationist camp. When William Jennings Bryan, the prosecutor in the case, could name only one scientist who shared his views, his case for the prosecution fizzled. Clarence Darrow, the criminal lawyer famous for his support of organized labor, defended Scopes, and although Scopes was found guilty, the press had ridiculed the prosecution, and in a few years the popularity of creationism faded.

Nevertheless, the creationists persisted, and they persuaded teachers and school boards to suppress any mention of evolution in the classroom. There was some success, and the creationists also formed their own societies and published their own journals. This effort was thwarted by a lack of trained scientists. However, in 1963, the Creation Research Society, in which members were required to have a graduate degree in a scientific discipline, was formed. They were also required to accept the inerrancy of the Bible, the special creation of all living things, and a world wide flood. Also, in the 1970s, the Institute for Creation Research was established in San Diego; it is presently the world's leading center for the propagation of creationism.[6]

Creationism faced a strong denial, however, in legal terms, when in 1987 the U.S. Supreme Court ruled that states that had sought to alter the science curriculum to reflect endorsement of a religious view antagonistic to the theory of evolution were breaking the First Amendment ban on the establishment of religion.[7] This ruling still prevails. It is evident that the support for creationism is gradually dwindling.

· · · · ·

CHAPTER 2 REFERENCES

1. "Creationism." *The New Encyclopedia Britannica.* 3: 721, 1994.
2. Metzger, B.M., and Murphy, R.E. *The New Annotated Bible.* Oxford University Press, Inc., New York, 1989, p. 3.
3. Numbers, R. L. *The Creationists.* Alfred A. Knopf, Inc., New York, 1992, p. 7.
4. "Creationism." *The Encyclopedia Americana.* 8: 164, 1998.
5. Numbers, R. L. Ibid., p. 62.
6. "Creationism." *The Encyclopedia Americana.* 8: 165, 1998.
7. "Creationism." *The New Encyclopedia Britannica.* 3: 721, 1994.

3

All life is kin.

Evolution

THE GRAND STORY OF THE 20TH CENTURY has been evolution. It sweeps all before it. It is awash with evidence that is both irrefutable and reproducible. The evidence continues to accumulate. It has transformed biology, and it has escalated from the pedestrian status of a theory to the higher ground of a fact. When Darwin's book on evolution was published, the gentle, reserved, English landowner became a world celebrity. It was not his wish; he couldn't avoid it. Possibly no other individual in the long corridor of history has ever changed society in such a pronounced and enduring way.

When Darwin returned to England at the end of his five year trip around the world on the Beagle, he brought with him voluminous notes and a large number of specimens. The purpose of his trip, as a naturalist, was simply to learn what he could. His observations from the trip lay fallow in his laboratory for a number of years. During this time he read Malthus and was introduced to the idea that animals overbreed their food supply, and on this account, some necessarily die. That is to say, only the fittest survive.

It was after the Beagle returned from the long voyage that Darwin put together the main ideas of his theory. Species overbreed their food supply; species produce variations in their offspring; and, those with variations most suitable to their environment survive, while the others do not. The former will pass along their favorable hereditary characteristics to the next generation, while the latter will not. It is, therefore, natural selection and overbreeding that allow the fittest to survive. Darwin concluded that small inherited changes winnowed by natural selection over long periods of time would account for speciation. Furthermore, Darwin believed that species are not created for any special purpose, or as part of any universal design.[1]

Darwin was urged to write. It took him 13 months and 10 days to complete, *On the Origin of Species by Natural Selection,* which appeared on the English newsstands on November 24, 1859. The first printing of 1,250 copies sold out on the first day! Readers understood Darwin to say that man evolved from apes, and controversy immediately followed. After all, evolution contradicted the popular story of creation as told in the Bible. The public now faced a grand question: should it believe in Darwin's evolution, or in the Bible's account which posited that the earth and all its inhabitants were formed in six days? Both could not be true.

It was a fascinating controversy. Darwin was ridiculed. In support of creationism, Bishop Ussher of Ireland insisted that the world was born in 4,004 B.C. Also in support was the Reverend Paley, who believed that so fine a structure as the human eye could not have been made by chance, and therefore, God must exist. That is the "Doctrine of Ignorance," which says that anything that cannot be explained must be due to God's work. Darwin could find no example that could not have been formed by numerous successive slight modifications, including the human eye.

Bishop Wilberforce of Oxford, with impertinence at an important meeting, asked Darwin whether his grandmother or grandfather had descended from apes. At the meeting, Thomas Huxley spoke for Darwin, who was not present. He replied to the Bishop that he would rather be descended from an ape than be a man who was afraid to face the truth. Consternation reigned. Never before had a bishop been thus insulted in public.

Finally, the "monkey trial," as the Scopes trial was called, occurred in 1925 in Dayton, Tennessee. This was mentioned in the preceding section on creationism. It has been said that "science after Darwin would no longer be able to call upon the miraculous to explain the workings of the natural universe."[2] But even today, while evolution is not uniformly accepted, explanations of the birth of the earth and the major biologic changes that followed are improved. It is useful to review these because it puts into perspective the whole story and shows the place of evolution in the grand biological scheme of things.

The great story is arbitrarily divided into ten biologic events. These take place over a span of time so long it can hardly be conceived. The span is over four thousand million years! That's when the earth formed. Just think of it. A million years is ten consecutive blocks of one hundred thousand years each! The lay concept of history goes back only about ten thousand years when civilization began. Christianity goes back only about two thousand years. A block of time of 100,000 years is staggering, and there are ten of them in each of the million years. There are over four thousand of the million years! The greatest difficulty in understanding evolution is in comprehending the amount of time over which the process took place.

We know this to be true because around the turn of the century, about 1900, radioactivity was discovered. Radioactive elements were found to decay at different rates that are constant. Moreover, the rate is absolutely unique for each element. Therefore, measuring the rate of decay identifies the element. When uranium, the heaviest of all the natural elements decays, it turns into lead, which is not radioactive. The half-life of uranium, which is the time it takes any number of atoms of the element to decay, is over four thousand million years. A "decay" is when an atom kicks out a part of its nucleus or a part of its shell of electrons (that's what radioactivity is). Therefore, the proportions of uranium and lead in rock provide a way to calculate the age of the rock. From such studies it was found that the earth is close to four thousand six hundred million years old.

A prominent idea of how the earth was formed is that the whole solar system, that is, the sun and planets, began as a cold cloud of dust of unimaginably large size. All the matter of the universe came from the "big bang," which happened about 16 billion years ago. What preceded that no one knows, yet. This is where some cite a Supreme Being who gave the force. Why that should seem like the natural answer is obscure.

To continue, the cloud separated into swirling masses that rotated and condensed to form the planets and the sun. Only the sun was large enough and dense enough to become so hot from gravitational compression that the thermonuclear reaction converting hydrogen to helium turned on. It was this reaction that turned matter into heat and light, and it was then that a new star began to shine in the sky. Planet formation may be common; recent evidence indicates that perhaps a third of stars comparable to our sun may already have planets.[3] However, the sun will not last forever. It has been there for about five billion years, with about another five billion to go, but fuel is gradually used up, and all stars burn out and die sometime. Their lives are finite.

Now for a little perspective. If the earth were reduced to a sphere the size of a basketball, the outermost crust would only be as thick as a coat of shellac. In the beginning, masses of space debris, some so large as to be termed "worldlets," crashed into the new earth causing massive craters on the surface and creating heat in the center. The innards of the earth became molten and began to glow a dull dark red. The heavy elements like iron and nickel, and the rare elements such as gold, platinum, and iridium, as well as the radioactive elements, sank deep into the mantle while the lighter elements made up the outer crust. This process of layering is called differentiation.

The earth was still young when the most catastrophic collision occurred. There never had been anything like it. A huge interstellar mass crashed into the earth, perhaps at a glancing blow, and knocked an enormous chunk of earth substance off into space. If the impact had been direct, it would have broken the earth into careening parts staggering off into space, resulting in the end of the earth. But it held together; the ejected mass formed a gravitational focus, swept in other debris, became round, and formed the moon.

Such a story might seem imaginative, but the moon expedition brought back rocks that had the same composition as the earth rocks. Moreover, studies of radioactivity revealed that the moon rocks also had an age of four thousand six hundred million years.

When the new earth returned to roundness after this tremendous disfiguring impact, it was still struck by space debris of various sizes so that many craters, large and small, marred the surface. The surface was a sea of pockmarks. With the passage of hundreds of millions of years, however, the sharp edges were gradually rounded off; mountain building erased some of the craters, running water, volcanic eruptions, tectonic plate movements, and the expansion of ice smoothed the surface so that eventually the crater marks all but disappeared. The moon was, of course, bombarded by the same chunks of debris, but without sufficient gravity to hold an atmosphere, no running water or ice expansion were available to modify the surface. Thus, the moon craters remain, and are visible and clear even with a telescope of low power.

In this way it happened: the earth was born. It was a time of gigantic collisions, catastrophic impacts, and unbelievable violence. Still it happened, and there it stood, ready for the next step in its evolution.

First, a way of visualizing these events is to construct a time scale with ten entries and the approximate number of years between events. The letters mya stand for million years ago. The numbers are, of course, approximate. The first event has already been described: the formation of the earth.

THE FIRST EVENT
1. 4,600 ... mya ... Earth forms
2.
3.
4.
5.
6.
7.
8.
9.
10.

THE SECOND EVENT
1. 4,600 ... mya ... Earth forms
2. 4,000 ... mya ... Molecules replicate
3.
4.
5.
6.
7.
8.
9.
10.

The second event, in some ways, was the most glorious of all. It was the beginning of life. What a moment it must have been! It took about 500 million years for certain things to happen. The molten red-glowing earth had to cool. That took a long time. Then the vapor from surface eruptions had to accumulate, and ice masses bombarding the earth had to vaporize into water. The rains came and the oceans formed. As the millions of years passed, water came to cover 70 per cent of the earth's surface. There the earth was, quiet and lifeless, a mass of land and water held together by gravity in an orbit around the sun. It was just sitting there. Fortunately, the orbit was just right; farther out and the water would have frozen, and closer in, the water would have boiled and evaporated. It is water that makes life possible.

Organic molecules are composed of carbon with other elements attached. They make up all living things. It turns out that the primitive oceans were rich in organic molecules. These included long-chain hydrocarbons, amino acids that are the building blocks of protein, methane, carbon dioxide, nitrogen, and nucleotide bases. Over a period of one or two hundred million years, these various molecules, floating about in the limitless oceans, connected with each other, disconnected, reattached to something else, and then separated again. The molecules in their various combinations, jostled about, finding all sorts of alignments. After millions and millions of years, it happened.

No one was there to see it, and no one was there to understand what it meant. It may have happened at several places at more or less the same time, but at some absolute moment, at some specific site, all that time ago and by pure chance, a molecule formed that had the astonishing capability of replicating itself. It could reproduce itself! At that moment the unstoppable surge of biology was born. From that moment on, nothing could stop the onrushing avalanche of living things. It was, by any measure, the greatest moment in the history of the earth. A kind of thrill attaches to the realization that this took place.

The molecule that could reproduce itself may have been ribonucleic acid, or RNA.[4] Its structure is shown in Figure A.

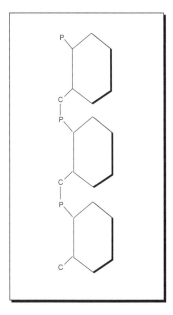

Fig. A. The six sided structures are ribonucleic acids connected to each other by links of phosphorus and carbon (P-C).

It wasn't very complicated, but nevertheless, it could reproduce itself. After more millions of years, by a process of evolutionary refinement, the RNA molecule transformed itself into a double-chained structure or DNA. Those letters stand for deoxyribonucleic acid. As is now commonly known, DNA is the master molecule of life. It also reproduces itself, in this manner. (Fig. B) The elongated double-sided chain may be thought of as a ladder.

Fig. B. The DNA ladder with its sides and rungs. The six-sided structures are now deoxyribonucleic acids (ladder), and the bases (rungs) are adenine, thymine, cytosine, and guanine. These are represented by the letters ATGC. A is always connected to T, and G is always connected to C. The ladder twists into a double helix.

With these developments, the biosphere was launched and underway. All of the leaves, flowers, grasses, weeds, sedges, brambles, bushes, trees, and forests, and all of the worms, whales, cats, warthogs, snakes, elephants, scorpions, and eagles, in short, all of the living things in the plant and animal kingdoms, are composed of cells. All of the cells have nuclei, and all of the nuclei have DNA. DNA is the master molecule of life. With this central invariant feature, all springing from the primitive oceans of the world, it may be realized that all life is related. Everything that lives has its instructions for life registered in its DNA. It should be said again: All life is related.

Everyone, including the creationist, asks: Where did the organic molecules come from that started this whole process? This is the point at which some insert the theory of a Supreme Being, those who believe in a divine Being but understand that science is fact.

Of course, there were elements in the water, on the land, and in the sea, such as hydrogen, oxygen, and nitrogen, and such primitive molecules as carbon dioxide and methane. No special formation was required for these. As to the source of the organic molecules, there are two possibilities. The first is that the effect of lightning, aural electrons from the sun, natural radioactivity, temperature changes from erupting volcanoes, and the impact of meteorites smashing onto the earth, caused organic molecules to form.

This is not just speculation. In 1953 Stanley Miller, then professor of biochemistry at the University of California, subjected an artificial atmosphere of ammonia, methane, carbon dioxide, and water vapor to electrical discharges and produced amino acids and long-chain hydrocarbons.[5] Thus, organic molecules may have been formed by natural forces working on indigenous materials.

The second possibility is that the organic molecules were delivered to earth by comets or meteorites. By 1985, 74 amino acids had been found in bodies that came from space. Of these, eight were associated with protein synthesis in living systems, 11 were of biological significance, and 55 were not found on earth.[6] So it is not clear whether the organic molecules were formed on earth, delivered to the earth, or both. If they were delivered to earth, the possibility of life elsewhere in the universe is raised.

THE THIRD EVENT
1. 4,600 ... mya ... Earth forms
2. 4,000 ... mya ... Molecules replicate
3. 3,000 ... mya ... Photosynthesis, chloroplasts
4.
5.
6.
7.
8.
9.
10.

The next event took a thousand million more years to develop. Imagine, a thousand million years. It was the transformation of molecules in the protective seas to intact cells that could also divide. The first cells had DNA, but no nuclei, and were known as prokaryotes, meaning "before nuclei." After millions of years, the cells walled off their internal DNA and formed nuclei. They were then known as eukaryotes meaning "normal nuclei." The first eukaryotes were unattached and were floating about in the seas altogether aimlessly.

While this was happening, another development was taking place. It was the formation of bacteria. There were many kinds. Bacteria have DNA, but no nuclei. These bacteria, in their countless hordes, developed in various ways, and one species took on a special skill. It learned how to take carbon dioxide and water, and make sugar and oxygen out of them. The process is powered by sunlight and is known as photosynthesis. It is the basis of all life on earth. That is the key reaction of all biology;

nothing could live without it. The sugar was used for nutrition, and the oxygen was given off as a waste gas. The bacteria, of course, had no idea of the importance of their new capability.

More millions of years passed and the bacteria in the oceans faced a grave problem. If they rose too close to the surface, they would be killed by the searing ultraviolet light; and, if they went too deep into the ocean, they would not get enough light to power their photosynthesis. They were caught in the middle, so to speak, and the problem for them was extremely serious.

One day an adventuresome bacterium did a remarkable thing; it nuzzled up to a passing nucleated cell, squeezed inside, and began to manufacture sugar and oxygen. The oxygen was given off as a waste, and the sugar was used for nourishment of the cell. This worked well because the cell wall protected the bacterium from the ultraviolet light, while at the same time the cell wall was sufficiently translucent to allow in enough sunlight to power the photosynthesis. So it was an agreeable arrangement; the cell benefitted from free nutrition, and the bacterium was protected from the ultraviolet light. It was a symbiotic relationship since both parties benefited from the same arrangement.

The relationship flourished, and it depended on chlorophyll. Chlorophyll is green, and it is found in the photosynthetic bacteria. The specific structures are chloroplasts, and the cells of all green plants have them.

Chloroplasts and photosynthesis are critical to life. Thus, the animal kingdom depends on the plant kingdom for food, and the plant kingdom depends on the chloroplasts for life, so these little structures are known as the "engines of life." We know that these little structures inside the cells of plants came from bacteria because these little chloroplasts carry their own DNA, and it is different from the DNA in the nucleus of the cell. That's how it became certain that the chloroplasts originally came from bacteria.

THE FOURTH EVENT.
1. 4,600 ... mya ... Earth forms
2. 4,000 ... mya ... Molecules replicate
3. 3,000 ... mya ... Photosynthesis, chloroplasts
4. 2,000 ... mya ... Oxygen, mitochondria
5.
6.
7.
8.
9.
10.

The fourth event was a great one. After the chloroplasts were in place as we described, the green cells with their chlorophyll and their photosynthesis began to proliferate. The cells formed great masses of phytoplankton that were large enough to turn vast areas of the ocean surface green. In all of these cells, the little metabolic engines were busy generating sugar on the one hand, and oxygen as a waste gas on the other. The oxygen, of course, was given off to the atmosphere, and it began to accumulate. Time went on by the millions of years and the oxygen continued to accumulate. A thousand million years passed and the concentration of oxygen in the atmosphere eventually reached about 20 per cent. That is to say, every fifth molecule in the atmosphere was oxygen. And that's the way it is today.

It turns out that oxygen is toxic. It is poisonous for organic things. It also damages inorganic structures like steel which, as a consequence of oxidation, rusts. Living organisms, aside from plants, also suffer from it. They die. With an atmosphere of 20 per cent oxygen, there was lots of death. It was an oxygen holocaust.

Then, once again, bacteria came to the rescue. A certain

species of bacteria learned to cope with oxygen. Therein lay the solution. Some of these bacteria sidled up to the eukaryotic cells, invaded them, and came to rest in the cytoplasm somewhere between the nuclear membrane and the external cell wall. Thereafter, the cells so equipped could handle oxygen and thus survive. So the practice spread, and even in the presence of oxygen the cells grew and were strong. Moreover, the tiny inclusions carried their own unique DNA and were able to reproduce right along with the reproduction of the cells. The inclusions became permanent, and they are known today as mitochondria. They corrected the sensitivity to oxygen and put an end to the oxygen holocaust. We owe much to bacteria.

Now an interesting relationship developed. The plants produce oxygen which the animals need to breathe, and the animals produce carbon dioxide which the plants need in their photosynthesis to produce more oxygen. So the plants produce a waste that the animals need, and the animals produce a waste that the plants need. It is the atmosphere that connects these two kingdoms in a grand symbiosis.

THE FIFTH EVENT
1. 4,600 ... mya ... Earth forms
2. 4,000 ... mya ... Molecules replicate
3. 3,000 ... mya ... Photosynthesis, chloroplasts
4. 2,000 ... mya ... Oxygen, mitochondria
5. 1,400 ... mya ... Plants colonize land
6.
7.
8.
9.
10.

Six hundred million years pass. The primitive sea is burgeoning with life. It is time for the plants to go ashore. Tentatively at first, they move onto land. The conditions are clement, and the plants thrive. By 1,400 million years ago the land has been colonized. The weeds, bushes, legumes, flowers, grasses, trees, and forests are all in place. A lush green carpet lies over the land. In a biologic sense, the life of the earth with its water and sunlight and nourishing soil, is well underway.

THE SIXTH EVENT
1. 4,600 ... mya ... Earth forms
2. 4,000 ... mya ... Molecules replicate
3. 3,000 ... mya ... Photosynthesis, chloroplasts
4. 2,000 ... mya ... Oxygen, mitochondria
5. 1,400 ... mya ... Plants colonize land
6. 1,300 ... mya ... Sex accelerates evolution
7.
8.
9.
10.

Another 100 million years pass, and one of the great biological shifts of all time takes place. It was the advent of sex. Up to that time, cells divided by simple fission. That is, they duplicated their own DNA and then split in two, with half of the original matter going to each of the parts. In this process, neither of the parent cells was left to die, and there were no new cells to replace them. Instead, there were only repeated divisions of some original cell. This went on for hundreds of millions of years. The process is seen in Figure C.

In this process of fission in which the DNA undergoes no change except to replicate and then divide, each of the offspring cells is exactly like the parent cell. There is no chance for varia-

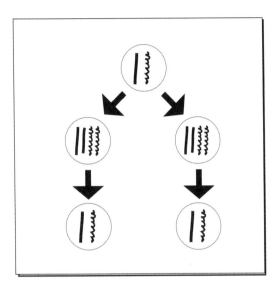

Fig. C. The vertical lines represent chromosomes which are in the nuclei of the cells and contain DNA. The offspring cells are exact copies of the original cell.

tion except for an occasional mutation. It turns out that DNA is an extremely complex molecule with billions of rungs in its ladder, and since mutations are random events, they are almost always harmful. It would be like jabbing a needle into a finely tuned watch and expecting the movement to improve.

Progress thus depended on advantageous mutations which are extremely rare, and this made evolutionary change agonizingly slow. Without genetic variation, animal life could not adapt to the environmental changes that were taking place all around it. Animal life was in a precarious situation, indeed.

Sex replaced this simple mechanism about 1,300 million years ago. The significance of sex was that it speeded up the evolutionary process. The reason is that sex allowed for a random shuffling of chromosomes between the maternal and paternal parties to a union. Incidentally, the number of chromosomes in the cells of various living things is both different and unique. For example: cats have 38 chromosomes per cell; humans 46; plums 48; dogs 78; goldfish 94; corn 20; cabbage 18; and mosquitoes 6.[7] All living things have them.

There are two kinds of cells in the body, somatic cells and sex cells. The former are the ordinary ones present in heart, lungs, gut, brain, muscle, liver, bone, and spleen. Sex cells are found only in the testes of men and the ovaries of women. In the somatic cells, division takes place by mitosis in which the chromosomes reproduce themselves and then divide without error so that the offspring cells have exactly the same genetic content as the parent cell. The degree of precision in this process is amazing, considering how large and how complex the DNA molecule is. The process is very much like fission that was previously described.

But the divisional process is different in the sex cells, which are the sperm in the male, and the ova in the female. When these cells divide, the genetic material or DNA, is divided in two with half from each parent going to the offspring. Thus, in the offspring the full amount is restored. This halving of the parental chromosomes is a reduction process and it is known as meiosis. We can draw this division, but for simplification just show two of the 46 chromosomes in the human cell.

Meiosis thus allows for a reshuffling of maternal and paternal DNA in the offspring cells. The shuffling of chromosomes is altogether random. Sex was thus fundamental to evolution because it provided a way to mix the genetic material from the parents, which gave variability to the offspring, and that allowed for natural selection to favor those inherited features that were advantageous.

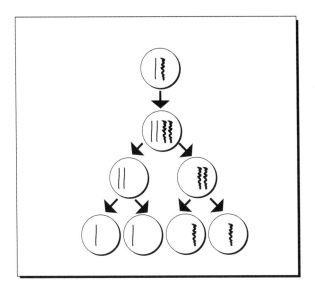

Fig. D. In meiosis or germ cell division, the offspring cells have only half of the genetic material from each parent. When these join with the germ cells of the opposite sex, the full complement of genetic material is restored. Straight chromosomes are paternal, squiggly ones are maternal.

This may be foreseen by the union of an attractive female animal who is heavy set with a slim male animal who is unattractive. Two issues of this union could be an attractive male who is slim, and an unattractive female who is heavy set. This shows that the genetic material (DNA) is mixed from the parents and passed on to the offspring.

When it is realized that this process of chromosome reshuffling was occurring throughout the animal world, and it continued for millions and millions of years, it is no wonder that pronounced variations in animal life eventually developed. This is the point at which evolution in the Darwinian sense began. It is here that Darwin changed our understanding of the varieties of animals that roamed the land.

The bottom line is that natural selection is a great sieve, straining out most with unfavorable inherited characteristics, and permitting those without such defects to continue. Over immense periods of time, continuing natural selection may bring about such a divergence of an organism from its parental stock as to constitute a new species.[8] Evolution is thus the interplay of heredity and environment. Ernst Mayr, the distinguished zoologist from Harvard University, is reported to have called this one of the most novel and most daring conceptualizations in the history of ideas.[9]

THE SEVENTH EVENT
1. 4,600... mya... Earth forms
2. 4,000... mya... Molecules replicate
3. 3,000... mya... Photosynthesis, chloroplasts
4. 2,000... mya... Oxygen, mitochondria
5. 1,400... mya... Plants colonize land
6. 1,300... mya... Sex accelerates evolution
7. 550... mya... Animals go ashore
8.
9.
10.

While the land was being colonized by plant life, the animals were still at sea developing at their own slow rate. The time came for them to go ashore, too. But there was a problem. When the animals came out on land, they were fried by the searing rays of the ultraviolet light. The land was not safe. However, the plants already ashore, and those in the oceans too, continued to produce oxygen through their photo-synthetic activity, and the effect of sunlight on oxygen is to produce ozone. It is ozone that blocks the ultraviolet rays of the sun and protects the land from their harmful effects. Millions of years passed and the oxygen continued to accumulate and the ozone continued to form. By and by it came to form a shield, and it is this that allowed the animals to go ashore and onto land safely. The attempts of sea life to go ashore rather suddenly succeeded, and the animals, now safely on land, established themselves, and began those adaptations that would provide them with comfort in their new environment.

THE EIGHTH EVENT
1. 4,600... mya... Earth forms
2. 4,000... mya... Molecules replicate
3. 3,000... mya... Photosynthesis, chloroplasts
4. 2,000... mya... Oxygen, mitochondria
5. 1,400... mya... Plants colonize land
6. 1,300... mya... Sex accelerates evolution
7.   550... mya... Animals go ashore
8.   270... mya... Continents move
9.
10.

The eighth event deals with the land masses that interrupt the seas. It began with Pangaea, a single, hypothetical, gigantic land mass that straddled the equator. There were no continents, there was only one land mass of enormous size. Now down in the middle of the earth, extending up to the mantle, there were radioactive elements that decayed spontaneously and generated large amounts of heat. The heat powered the slow cycling of the molten mantle, and this caused the overlying thin crust of earth to shift and move and buckle.

Such movement, of course, affected Pangaea. It broke into a

northern component, called Laurasia, which consisted of North America, Greenland, Northern Europe, Russia, Siberia, and a part of Southern Europe, and a southern component known as Gondwanaland, that consisted of Antarctica, Australia, Africa, China, and India.[10] These two huge land masses then broke up into the separate continents that we know today. Of course, it didn't happen overnight. It was extremely gradual. In fact, the rate of movement of these various land masses was only one inch per year.

THE NINTH EVENT
1. 4,600... mya... Earth forms
2. 4,000... mya... Molecules replicate
3. 3,000... mya... Photosynthesis, chloroplasts
4. 2,000... mya... Oxygen, mitochondria
5. 1,400... mya... Plants colonize land
6. 1,300... mya... Sex accelerates evolution
7. 550... mya... Animals go ashore
8. 270... mya... Continents move
9. 245... mya... Permian extinction
10.

Number nine is also astonishing. It's known as the great Permian die-off. It occurred about 245 million years ago, and it was due to a major climatic disturbance in which volcanic activity erupted all over the world. Most of the land was covered with hot volcanic ash. Most of the animals died. The plants died. Ninety five per cent of every living thing on earth died.[11] It was a near wipe-out. It was the greatest mass-death ever seen on earth. It was the Permian extinction.

The cause of this catastrophe was a spasm of activity in the mantle of the earth where the radioactive elements heat the earth substance into a molten mass. Had the spasm been more pronounced, all life could have been extinguished. From this it hardly appears that there was a grand design to nature.

It took about ten million years to recover from the catastrophe. In talking about hundreds of millions of years, ten doesn't seem like so much. To speak about ten million years, think of a dime. It's about one millimeter in thickness. The tallest mountain in the world is Mt. Everest. It's almost six miles straight up to the top. Now if wind and ice and weather wear off the top of that mountain at the rate of one millimeter per year, in ten million years Mt. Everest would be worn down flat to sea level. Ten million years is an enormous amount of time.

Nevertheless, the long time passed, and the earth recovered. Slowly, of course, but the growth of plants did resume, the animals repopulated the land, and gradually the whole biosphere returned to its pre-Permian condition. The biologic adventures were ready to continue.

THE TENTH EVENT
1. 4,600... mya... Earth forms
2. 4,000... mya... Molecules replicate
3. 3,000... mya... Photosynthesis, chloroplasts
4. 2,000... mya... Oxygen, mitochondria
5. 1,400... mya... Plants colonize land
6. 1,300... mya... Sex accelerates evolution
7. 550... mya... Animals go ashore
8. 270... mya... Continents move
9. 245... mya... Permian extinction
10. 65... mya... Dinosaur die-off

In the 1970s, Walter Alvarez was studying rock layers in Gubbio, Italy. One of the layers, formed 65 million years ago, was black. It was only a half inch thick and it was a mystery to him. He bombarded the black layer with neutrons which made the black material radioactive. Analysis of the radioactivity then revealed that the black material was iridium, and it was 30 times more concentrated than expected. Still puzzled, he packaged up his specimen and brought it home to his father, Louis Alvarez, who was a Nobel Laureate in physics at the University of California, Berkeley.

Louis Alvarez knew at once what had happened. When the earth differentiated into core, mantle, and crust, the heavy elements of iron and nickel went to the core and carried with them the noble elements of gold, osmium, and iridium. On this account, iridium is scarce in the earth's crust. Meteorites, however, have not gone through the differentiation process so that their iridium is mixed evenly within their substance. Therefore, if a meteor had hit the earth and become pulverized by the impact, a huge cloud of dust containing iridium would have gone up into the stratosphere and then settled into a single, uniform layer over the earth's surface.

Moreover, this would have happened at a specific time so that the iridium layer would be found only in one stratum of the earth's crust. All of that being reasonable, a search was undertaken to explore the critical rock layer wherever it was preserved. To 1994, over 100 sites of high iridium content in that layer had been found. The Alvarez explanation was published in Science, June 6, 1980.

It might be wondered where the iridium came from in the first place. As it happens, when stars die, they explode and the explosion is called a supernova. It is in that gigantic explosion that the heavy elements like iron and nickel, and the noble elements like gold and iridium are formed. The problem with the Alvarez explanation was that there was no crater to account for the iridium-producing explosion. It turned out that Pemex, which is the National Oil Company of Mexico, was looking for offshore oil in the Gulf of Mexico just off the Yucatan Peninsula.

A magnetic survey of the region, followed by a gravity survey, discovered a crater 100 miles in diameter. Then a drilling at the site brought up samples of "shocked quartz" which confirmed an extraterrestrial deposit.

Other studies, undertaken later, indicated that the crater might have been as large as 180 miles in diameter. An impact of that size would be the equivalent of a five billion megaton nuclear explosion.

The crater was five miles deep and at least 100 miles in diameter. It was the greatest earth impact since life originated on this planet. When it happened, hundreds of cubic miles of dust went up into the stratosphere. The impact created tidal waves a thousand feet high. Hurricane-force winds developed. The heat generated by this impact ignited fires the world over, and this was evidenced by a thin layer of soot in the same layer as the iridium. The dust, 400 cubic miles of it, blotted out the sun for months to as many as three years.

The earth fell into darkness, black as night. Temperatures dropped, and freezing occurred even at the equator. Photosynthesis was blocked, plants on land and sea died, and the ecosystem of the earth collapsed. No animal weighing over 50 pounds survived![12] It was a time of widespread death, not as great as the Permian extinction, but great nevertheless.

From the standpoint of evolution, there was a huge significance to this event. For 200 million years dinosaurs had ruled the land. Grotesque, lumbering, enormous meat-eating beasts, they were the ferocious and insatiable carnivores of the day. Among their prey were the early mammals which, at that time, were small rodent-sized animals hiding in the forests, cowering in the shadows, and venturing out to hunt only at night. Suddenly, the great carnivores were gone.

The mammals now gained confidence, they emerged from their hiding places and began to mature. From that time on they developed, grew in size, learned to walk upright, and their brains enlarged. Mammalian development, leading to the appearance of early human beings, was the main evolutionary consequence of the dinosaur extinction.[13] The great beasts were gone forever. It should be mentioned that this explanation of the dinosaur extinction is not uniformly accepted.[14]

After the dinosaur die-off, 65 million years passed. During that time new species of animals appeared, old species matured, and some species became extinct. Also, some learned new tricks. Primitive humans began to appear, land animals learned to live in the sea, and others learned to fly in the air. It attests to the adaptability of life that some live on land, some in the sea, and some in the air. Life loves itself, and it will find a way to exist, and even thrive, in virtually any environment.

Prehuman animals came from reptilian stock some 200 million years ago.[15] The primitive forms coexisted with dinosaurs until 65 million years ago when the great animals disappeared. When that happened, the mammals came forward, grew up, matured, and began to dominate the land. The early primates were characterized by five-digit extremities, nails rather than claws, and freely moveable limbs. They hunted for food. Hunting couldn't support a growing population in one place so the choice for the hunters was hard; they had to move or starve. Thus, they became hunter-gatherers. They moved about in bands of various sizes looking for food and other sustenance.

Then a most wonderful thing happened. Haltingly at first, the early humans learned to grow their own food. As their skills increased, agriculture appeared. It happened about 10,000 years ago. Now the nomadic tribes could come to rest. They could settle down at one place and develop their own resources. There was a sense of permanence and location. This necessitated some new habits and rules. The roving tribes had to accustom themselves to communal living. Rules for civil order had to be formulated.

Cooperative ventures had to be developed. In short, civilization began, and it was the discovery of agriculture that made it possible.

In a way, agriculture could be described as the eleventh event, but it was a human development rather than a major biologic change. That's why it's not included in the ten great biologic events over which man had no control.

There are at least two observations to be made. The first is that the dominance of evolution over creationism is so great as to make the latter doubtful; and, if that is so, then the Bible is in error. If the Bible is in error on this matter, then it may be in error on other matters. Thus, the literal word of the Bible is proven suspect. The conclusion is that man is probably alone on the crust of this minor planet, and he will have to solve the problems he faces because there is no one else to solve them. He will have to take charge of his own destiny.

◆ ◆ ◆ ◆ ◆

CHAPTER 3 REFERENCES

1. Durant, J., Editor. *Darwin and Divinity*. Basil Blackwell, Inc., New York, 1985, p. 26.

2. Jastrow, R. General Editor. *The Essential Darwin*. Masters of Modern Science Series. Little, Brown, and Company, Boston, 1948, p. vii.

3. Jastrow, R. *Red Giants and White Dwarfs*. W. W. Norton & Company Inc., New York, 1990, p. 95.

4. Sagan, C., and Druyan, A. *Shadows of Forgotten Ancestors*. Random House, New York, 1992, p. 94.

5. Curtis, H., and Barnes, N.H. *Invitation to Biology*, Fourth Edition. Worth Publishers, New York, 1985, p. 56.

6. Norton, O.R. *Rocks from Space*. Mountain Press Publishing Co., Missoula, Montana, 1994, p. 198.

7. Curtis, H., and Barnes, N.H. Ibid., p. 155.

8. Sagan, C., and Druyan, A. Ibid., 1992.

9. Lewin, R. "Thread of Life." *The Smithsonian Looks at Evolution*. W.W. Norton & Company, New York, 1982, p. 44.

10. Curtis, H., and Barnes, N.H. Ibid., p. 544.

11. Lewin, R. Ibid., p. 165.

12. Sagan, C., and Druyan, A. Ibid., p. 164.

13. Ibid., p. 141.

14. Lewin, R. Ibid., p. 165.

15. Ibid., p. 163.

4

The evidence mounts.

Molecular Evolution

THE EVIDENCE FOR EVOLUTION has been mainly the similarity of skeletal features between present day structures and fossil remains. This is known as comparative morphology. The second method is the carbon dating of fossils that reveal when they were alive. These have been the main ways of establishing the past record of life on earth. Now a third method has become available. It is known as molecular anthropology, and what it does is to compare the DNA in the cells of various species now alive with those that became extinct long ago. What this shows is that all animals are related, and approximately when the branchings of the tree of life took place.

There are three billion rungs in the ladder of the DNA, and these rungs are in every single cell. In fact, the three billion rungs are in the nucleus of every cell, and that's even smaller. The DNA ladder of the monkey is 99 per cent identical with that of the human. In order to make that statement, it is necessary to compare the DNA ladders of the monkey and the human.

If you put a single human cell, or a single monkey cell for that matter, on a paper, it would be so small that it would be barely visible to the unaided eye. Each one of these cells has three billion rungs in its DNA ladders; these rungs have been compared between species.

What the scientists found is called DNA typing. It's the most powerful way of discovering genetic variation among different species or among individuals of the same species.[1] The technique is basically quite simple. First, let me show you how the sides of the DNA ladder are composed of phosphorus and sugar molecules that alternate. (Fig. E) The sugar is deoxyribose. The rungs of the ladder are made of four bases, Adenine (A), Thymine (T), Cytosine (C), and Guanine (G). Adenine and thymine always pair together, and cytosine only pairs with guanine. It is interesting that all living things, plant and animal, are governed by DNA, and all of the DNA in the whole world is made up of just these six structures: sugar, phosphorus, and four bases.

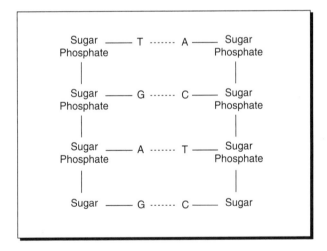

Fig. E. The sides of the DNA ladder are alternating molecules of sugar and phosphorus. The rungs of the ladder are the four bases: A, T, G, and C. The dots between the bases indicate that they are easily separated from one another. The ladder is twisted to form a double helix, but for clarification is shown in straightened form.

In the human there are about three billion rungs in the DNA ladder so that it is an enormously long structure. It is composed of about 100,000 genes, each of which is simply a segment of the ladder. Special base sequences mark off the beginning and end of each gene. The sum total of all of the genes is the genome. Restriction enzymes are able to cut the DNA ladder at the beginning and ends of the genes. The material is then washed and placed in an agar gel to which a weak electric charge is applied. The genes, which are also electrically charged, migrate in the gel under the current, and sort themselves by size.

They are then labeled with a radioactive probe and set on an X-ray film which, when developed, shows the number, position, and size of the genes. This pattern is specific for the individual, and comparison of this pattern with that of others clarifies such useful matters as lineage in paternity suits, and identifies criminals in other matters. It also exonerates those wrongly accused of certain crimes.

There are two points in the molecular methods that show the relatedness of animals and fossils. The first is that the DNA structure does remain intact over long periods. For example, the DNA sequence from Egyptian mummies has been read, as have those from a 40,000 year old mammoth, and an insect embedded in amber over twenty million years ago.[2]

The second point is that DNA typing is too expensive, too time-consuming, and too wasteful of laboratory resources to be useful in reading the DNA ladders of different animals. It's not an efficient method, but it is being used to map the entire human genome. That project will take years to complete; it will cost billions of dollars; and, it will require the collaboration of laboratories in several different countries. Right now in America, work is underway to map chromosomes four, seven, and eleven, as well as the X chromosome.[3] The whole international project is being coordinated by the Human Genome Organization which is known as HUGO. When completed, the map will be helpful in understanding such inherited human diseases as cystic fibrosis and sickle cell anemia.

That leaves the question of how to investigate the base-pair sequences in the DNA of various animal species. Through the ingenuity of the scientists, a partial answer to the problem has been found. To understand their solution, it is necessary to know that the ongoing business of the cell is to produce proteins. To do this, the DNA unzips right down the middle, and RNA (a substance like DNA except with ribose as the sugar) then comes in to copy the base sequence of the unzipped DNA. After the copying is completed, the DNA zips itself back together and resumes its usual form. The RNA, however, leaves the nucleus and takes its sequence (it's called a message) into the cytoplasm where it finds a ribosome. The ribosome picks up amino acids floating freely in the cytoplasm and hooks them together in the sequence of the RNA message. Since the RNA reflects the sequence of bases in the DNA, the sequence of amino acids in the new protein also reflects the sequence of bases in the DNA.

It's a lot easier to determine the amino acid order in a protein than it is to determine the sequence of three billion bases in the ladder of DNA. Scientists have found a protein in the serum of all oxygen-utilizing animals that has a constant number of 104 amino acids. It's called cytochrome c, and it's used in cellular respiration. The amino acid sequences of neurospora, moths, the screw worm, snakes, turtles, penguins, chickens, ducks, pigeons, kangaroos, rabbits, pigs, donkeys, horses, dogs, monkeys and man have been determined.[4] It was found that the sequences were similar for animals and man. Calling them "similar" is enough for an understanding, as this is not an exact scientific account of the matter. But, in this way it becomes clear that all animals, including the human, are related; all life is kin, and all of us are the evolutionary product of some common primordial ancestor that sprang into life some billions of years ago.

Based on this evidence, it does appear that we are all branches of the same evolutionary tree, and that evolution is mindless. Perhaps evolution appears directionless, but it is seen as ongoing.

• • • • •

CHAPTER 4 REFERENCES

1. Thro, E. *Genetic Engineering: Shaping the Materials of Life.* Facts on File, Inc., New York, 1993, p. 57.

2. Whitfield, P. *From So Simple a Beginning.* Macmillan Publishing Co., New York, 1993, p. 175.

3. Thro, E. Ibid, p. 93.

4. *NSF Mosaic Reader, Evolution, New Perspectives.* Avery Publishing Group, Inc., New Jersey, 1983, p. 23.

PART TWO

PART ONE REVEALED that evolution gives good account of the form and function of all living things. It also revealed that the divinity of Christ and the existence of God are unsupported by objective evidence. Without either, the natural question is: What does religion contribute? Of what use is it? It will be proper to examine this question, and to consider the favorable and unfavorable, if any, aspects of this concept that takes so much of our time and treasure. It will also be useful to look at alternative religions, and even those beliefs that do not, by definition, qualify as a religion.

◆ ◆ ◆ ◆ ◆

5

*Divinity and morality
are independent concepts.*

The Good, the Misleading, and the Doubtful

Religion is defined as belief in a supernatural being.[1] Since all religions have such beings, these include the Hindus, Muslims, Buddhists, Jews, and Christians. Under Christianity are the Catholics and Protestants, as well as subsets of the latter that include the Episcopalians, Methodists, Presbyterians, Mormons, Baptists, and Congregationalists. It appears that everyone needs a God to revere. They all do even though several are required to tithe; all are asked to contribute yearly; nearly all are exhorted to live moral lives under penalty of purgatory; and, by swearing allegiance to a presumed deity, all are promised unending paradise in a putative afterlife. It's so little to pay and so much to get that the promise is irresistible.

The largest of these religious groups are the Christians, and they will serve in this discussion. The basis of the Christian faith is a divine Christ and an extant God.

People want a deity. They want a haven after death, an eternal life in a heavenly paradise, which Christianity promises. They are told they can have this paradise by simply affirming God. Also, people want to be loved individually by God, and they are convinced that this is one of the rewards for believing. The proposition is extremely attractive; simple affirmation of God gives so much. The churches benefit, too, as they are much respected and held in the highest regard. So it's a win-win situation for religion. It can't fail. And finally, there's no way to disprove what the churches claim. It's no wonder religion is such a success.

However, many view the claims of religion as myth. If people want a myth to be true, and if the churches insist that the myth is true, and if the myth cannot be disproved, then the myth will be accepted as true. It will be taken as a fact, but it's still a myth. Then the question can be asked: Even if it is all myth, where is the harm?

The great religion of Christianity has three aspects that warrant comment. The first is the enormous good the churches provide for society. The second is the inextricable mix of divinity and morality that the churches proclaim, which is unintentionally misleading; and, the third is the selling of salvation, in which threat is used to extract money from the gullible. That churches benefit from this practice is undoubted, but the practice is questionable.

All over America there are hundreds of thousands of churches. Every community has at least one, and most have several. Most of these churches are small. The amount of good they do for society is incalculable. The ministers comfort the lonely, grieve with the bereaved, encourage contributions for charities, and give hope to the depressed.

The Sunday services are a comfort to the community. Other weekly services give support to the elderly, as well as to the young in the form of social events. The delivery of meals to the confined, and the provision of homes for girls with unplanned pregnancies are important services. Counseling for those in need, as well as officiating at marriages and funerals, are also necessary components of the ministerial services.

Moral leadership for the healthy and well adjusted is also a service. In large and small ways, conspicuous and obscure, the ministers of America go about their work emphasizing the moral path, assisting the unfortunate, and contributing in so many ways to the betterment of the community. Churches are a communal necessity, and this aspect of Christianity is wonderful and wholesome, and good.

In looking at the church services, it is seen that morality and divinity are mixed together. Thus, the singing of hymns, the benediction, the offertory, the prayers, the sermon, the communion, and the reading of scripture all affiliate with divinity. This is the misleading part. Without a God or a divine Christ, the connection with divinity is spurious.

There is a harm in the implication that morality is dependent on divinity. The Ten Commandments, for example, are moral instructions. They are said to be the words of God, and therefore, should be obeyed. There is no proof that they are the words of God; there is proof that they are the words of man. Moses said God spoke to him and gave them to him. That Moses promoted the Ten Commandments is history. God is not a reality in history. The commandments are not valuable because they are attributed to God; they are valuable because they are useful rules for wholesome communal living. They are independent of a church – Catholic, Protestant, Jewish, or otherwise.

The moral rules, the themes covered in the Ten Commandments, are necessary and important because a society without morality is not civilized. Moses sought to teach the Commandments to give direction to a society that was increasingly immoral in its behavior. The clergy teaches morality or "right living" in conjunction with it being the will of God or Allah, as though it depends on a belief in divinity to exist as a concept. The fact is that morality is a requirement of civilization.

It is critically necessary; whereas, divinity is totally superfluous. It should be the will of the people, of each individual, because civilized behavior is right behavior.

If it were broadly recognized that morality and divinity are independent of one another, and that only morality matters, then there would be no place for the church with its concentration on divinity. That is to say, morality can be taught, and good works can be provided, as well by atheists as by the devout. Churches amplify their usefulness by mixing the two parts of the message.

This is especially well shown by Catholicism, which functions through an elaborate hierarchy of orders that encompasses both morality and divinity. The two are mixed and entangled, not, of course, on purpose to preserve the place of the church. The Catholic church supports blind faith, allegiance to the organization which speaks for God. Morality is dictated, leaving nothing to chance.

At the top of the Catholic hierarchy is the pope. He is followed, in terms of authority, by the Vatican Secretary of State, and then by a succession of cardinals, archbishops, bishops, priests, deacons, and lesser functionaries. These supervise the many orders that include the Congregation for the Doctrine of the Faith (safeguards the doctrine of faith and morals), the Congregation for Bishops (oversees the jurisdiction of the bishops), the Congregation for Divine Worship and Discipline of the Sacraments (oversees promotion and regulation of the liturgy), the Congregation for the Causes of Saints (handles matters connected with beatification and canonization), the Congregation for the Clergy (concerned with the life, discipline, rights and duties of the clergy), the Congregation for the Institutes of Consecrated Life and Societies of Apostolic Life (competence over religious institutes, secular institutes, and societies of the apostolic life), the Congregation for Catholic Education (for

Seminaries and Institutes of Study), and the Congregation for the Evangelization of Peoples (directs missionary work throughout the world).

In the set-up are also three tribunals, and several councils. Among the latter are the Pontifical Council for the Laity, the Pontifical Council for promoting Christian Unity, the Pontifical Council for the Family, the Pontifical Council for the Justice of the Peace, the Pontifical Council for "Cor Unum," the Pontifical Council for the Pastoral Assistance to Health Care Workers, the Pontifical Council for the Interpretation of Legislative Texts, the Pontifical Council for Interreligious Dialogue, the Pontifical Council for Culture, and the Pontifical Council for Social Communications.

In addition, there are 20 commissions and committees. All of this inextricably mixes morality and divinity, and all of this is done for the administration of a religious denomination that lacks irrevocable evidence of a deity. A degree of doubt thus taints the whole enterprise. If there were a deity, would all of these positions be necessary for goodness through deity worship?

The present pope, Carol Wojtyla, was born as other mortals, devoted his life to the church, and at age 58 was appointed pope by his fellow cardinals. He took the name Pope Paul II, and several other names as well. He also took the prerogatives of his office, which include the right of infallibility. This means that his instructions are always correct and must be followed without question.

This concentration of authority in one man has a medieval ring to it. In the modern world, judgments are entrusted to the majority, and democracy is generally preferred to theocracy. There is also the danger that excessive authority will be abused. In his encyclical, entitled The Social Concerns of the Church, Pope John Paul II denounced the world's major powers – both capitalist and Marxist – for imposing their political and ideological views upon people in developing countries. He also denounced foreign aid that requires or promotes population control through artificial methods, such as birth control devices. These pronouncements indicate that Pope John Paul II does, in fact, regard himself as the spokesman for God, and he interprets his narrow views of Catholic doctrine as the only way for the faithful to think and behave, to the point of punishing those who question publicly or differ on points of conscience.

Other Christian religions have similar hierarchies from which to dictate the way their flocks should think and behave. Each has its chain of command, some with policy dictated from age old interpretation, and some with a democratic way of slowly changing policy.

Another aspect of Christianity that is suspect is the use of coercion to encourage the unannointed to join the fold, promising salvation. Then there is the practice of asking for money to continue the ministry. This is the province of the televangelists, and five are conspicuous for their outstanding success. They are Robert Schuller, Oral Roberts, Jerry Falwell, Pat Robertson, and Billy Graham.

Robert Schuller of Garden City, California, preaches self-esteem theology. His sermons emphasize how hurting people can be helped by prayer. The public is hungry for his feel-good, self-esteem message, and will pay to hear that message over and over again, so much so that he built a huge glass cathedral that is outfitted with sophisticated television equipment, and from which his sermons are beamed around the world.

He opens his Sunday service by saying that God loves those in front of him, and so does he, thus affiliating himself somehow with God. Schuller believes he speaks to God, and that God speaks to him.[2] He seems to consider himself as God's messenger, even though credible evidence that God exists is lacking.

Jerry Falwell was raised in a secular household in

Lynchburg, Virginia. He was captivated by stories of the Bible, decided to become a preacher, and gained salvation by admitting sin and accepting Christ. Falwell believed that life embraced two worlds, one of God, and one of man. He thought of life as a battlefield with God on one side and Satan on the other, taking Christ as his commander-in-chief, and the Bible as his guide in the war.

Falwell started the Thomas Road Baptist Church in Lynchburg in 1956. He believed that the salvation of the world depends on getting the word out.[3] He got the message out by radio and television. Falwell requested money and it was granted, enough to build an accredited university with graduate schools and a Seminary. He incorporated the Moral Majority in 1979 with a platform of pro-life, pro-family, pro-moral, and pro-America, carrying his message to the state capitals of the nation. It was rejected. He was scorned and went home to Lynchburg.

Today, Falwell continues with his hour-long television programs, no doubt with his plans to evangelize the nation. Jerry Falwell deserves credit for many good works. However, he speaks to God, claims God speaks to him, believes in the Second Coming of Christ, and in the inerrancy of the Bible. He appears to be naive in the sense that he thinks he knows what's best for others.

Oral Roberts, from a little town near Tulsa, Oklahoma, learned as a boy from a traveling preacher that disease could be cured by a laying on of hands. Soon thereafter, he had an audible call from God who told him to take a healing power to his generation, and to build a university. Roberts undertook healing crusades and the public responded in droves. Then he extended his message to millions via television, and donations were received in showers. One contained a check for a million dollars!

Roberts' main project was to build a university, which he did with 18 buildings on 400 acres in Tulsa. It opened in 1956, was dedicated by Billy Graham, and ran out of money in the mid-1980s. He went on television and claimed that if eight million dollars were not raised by a certain date, God would call him home. The media chuckled; Oral had made God an extortionist. The ploy flopped, and by 1989, the university closed. Roberts was sincere. He believed he was carrying the message of God to his followers. He spoke in tongues, believed in Satan and in the Second Coming of Christ. He believed he lived a supernatural life in a natural world.[4] Oral Roberts was a promoter who lost the confidence of his followers.

The fourth televangelist to mention is Marion Gordon 'Pat' Robertson who was born in 1930 to a father who was an ex-senator, and a mother who was a devout Christian. He attended Yale, and graduated from the New York Theological Seminary in l959. Without funds, he originated the 700 Club, bought television stations, and named his enterprise the Christian Broadcasting Network (CBN). He was soon reaching a million homes, formed a political group called the Freedom Council, and took over the leadership of the Christian Coalition. In 1988 Robertson ran for the presidency of the United States.

Robertson built one of the most powerful religious-political organizations in American history. He has far-right political views, and on this account has been regarded as dangerous to American democracy.[5] It is reported that he claims God talks to him, that he believes in Satan, that he calls on the government to form hit squads to assassinate terrorists, that he rails against evolution, and that he recommends religious tests for public office.[5] His run for president exposed him to a wary public who did not listen to his programs and had been unfamiliar with his teachings.

Billy Graham was born in Charlotte, North Carolina, and graduated from High School in 1936, which was the extent of his formal education. His first job was selling vacuum cleaners where he learned that sincerity is the biggest part of selling anything, including the Christian plan of salvation.[6] He excelled at revivals which were held all over the world before hundreds of thousands. He thought the devil was supernaturally counteracting Christianity.[7]

Graham taught that people are sinful and corrupt, that their sins may be absolved by accepting Jesus Christ as savior, and that acceptance will guarantee everlasting life in heaven. Also, that failure to accept Christ will doom them to an eternity in the fires of hell. In the Invitation, he asks his congregations to come forward and say that they want Christ in their hearts. If that is done, according to Graham, God will do the rest, and the rewards are beyond measure. Hundreds come forward, accept Christ, and crown his crusades with success.

It wasn't that Graham had anything new to say, it was just his profound sincerity. On one occasion he announced that people were going to hell because they were sinners.[8] He thus dispensed guilt on the one hand, and salvation on the other. But his revivals were enormously successful.

Graham regards himself as an evangelist and international diplomat, pointing out that he has discussed important questions with seven American presidents, other heads of state and world leaders, and more people searching for God than perhaps any man in history.[9] He believes in Satan, and in hell, and he thinks Adam and Eve were real people. He has said he is sure that the mother of Christ was a virgin.[10] He can be given to flattery, having signed a letter to President Eisenhower in which he stated that he thought of him as the greatest President in American history.[11] Billy Graham's skill as a preacher, his disarming humility, and his deep sincerity have carried him a long way.

The televangelists continue to make claims of faith sound like declarations of fact. Robert Schuller, Oral Roberts, and Billy Graham claim they have spoken with God. They also claim God has spoken to them. Pat Robertson and Jerry Falwell both claim they have received instructions from God. All claim that God performs miracles, and that the Bible is inerrant. The claims are not based on examinable facts. They have extracted millions upon millions of dollars from the public in the name of Christ, and have built successful religious businesses.

♦ ♦ ♦ ♦ ♦

CHAPTER 5 REPERENCES

1. "Religion." *American Heritage College Dictionary*, Third Edition. Houghton Mifflin Company, Boston, 1993.
2. Schuller, R. S. *Prayer: My Soul's Adventure with God. A Spiritual Autobiography.* Thomas Nelson, Inc., Nashville, 1995.
3. Falwell, J. *Strength for the Journey. An Autobiography.* Simon and Schuster, Inc., New York, 1987.
4. Hadden, J.K. and Shupe, A. *Televangelism. Power and Politics on God's Frontier.* Henry Holt and Company, New York, 1988.
5. Boston, R. *The Most Dangerous Man in America?* Prometheus Books, 1995.
6. Martin, W. *Prophet with Honor.* William Morrow and Company, Inc., New York, 1991, p. 67.
7. Ibid., p. 125.
8. Ibid., p. 156.
9. Ibid., p. 575.
10. Ibid., p. 578.
11. Ibid., p. 208.

6

*A postulate without
evidence is meaningless.*

Atheism

AN A-THEIST IS A PERSON WITHOUT THEISM, and theism is a belief in something supernatural. Those who do not believe in anything supernatural are atheists. There is no way to conclude that they do not believe in morality, however, and many are vocal about this fact. It is evident from these hundreds of thousands of individuals that morality can be taught without reference to theism. That is, theism and morality are altogether separate and independent of each other. So if we have two men who are equally moral, but only one believes in a supernatural body, would there be any difference between them? Reason would say not.

Speaking just for Christianity, a moral person would not be improved by thinking that Jesus was divine, that God exists, that virginal birth was possible, that Christ will return, or that Jesus performed miracles. There is no proof that a person is improved by these beliefs. That being so, there is no reason to scorn atheists, as some do. It harms no one not to believe in theism; that is, not to believe in the supernatural.

Of course, atheism is anathema to church thinking people. It means the atheist disavows what churches teach. If everyone were an atheist, there would be no need for churches. If everyone observed a moral code so that society were wholesome and stable, what would be the need for churches? Now, of course, there are those in society who do need friendship and consoling. Unexpected misfortune, a death of a loved one, loneliness, deep poverty, lack of family, and other conditions of remorse give individuals need for friendship, consolation, compassion, and comfort. But if these were provided, would it add anything to offer the ministrations of something supernatural?

What that does is to let the mind of the tormented wander into the surreal and suppose that a supernatural Being is, in fact, attending to the needs of the individual. This is easily supposed because the individual wants such attention, the theist vouches for the attention, and there is no way to refute the promises of the theist. It is comforting to the mind to believe in this unchallengeable faith.

Just to speculate freely: What if it became evident that theism were manufactured by man, that there is nothing supernatural? The atheist declares that there are no gods, no devils, no angels, no heaven or hell. There is only our natural world. To them, religion is but a myth and superstition that hardens hearts and enslaves minds. Whether or not this is true, there is no evidence to refute it.

The need for solace and comfort, however, is very real. It is also very frequent. It is a need that society must address. Many priests, ministers, rabbis, lesser dalai lamas, and other spiritual leaders do this work and call for God's help. Why, then, could not a system for compassionate persons who understand this need, are not diverted by theism, and not in a private practice of psychology or psychiatry be set up into official societies to provide relief from grief? They would console those who need to talk over their problems and need help finding solutions. It would be soothing and comforting.

They might organize groups who share the same grief so

that they could come together and commiserate. Those faced with divorce or family deaths, possibly alcoholics, perhaps drug addicts (especially in the young), and others disconsolate for any number of reasons might form such groups. Also, topics dealing with cultural and social injustice could be explored. That would be an important function in the community.

Those who would doubt the credibility of such an undertaking might ask themselves whether the grieving process is improved by praying to a supernatural Being. This is a valid question, especially when there is no evidence of such a Being, but so many find comfort in doing so. The fact is that there are organized community groups who do practice these concepts in a secular manner.

The theists, however, believe that such a Being exists, and prayer to that Being is valid. Fine. But can those who make this claim bring forward unassailable evidence that a supernatural Being exists? In that case, Christianity would not be a faith, it would be a fact. But it remains a faith because it is not validated by evidence. To be without faith is the conscious choice of many.

In all other subjects, when a postulate is put forward, it is up to the proponent to bring forward evidence to support the postulate. It is not up to the unenlightened to disprove the postulate. Were this not the case, anyone could postulate anything and no one could refute it. In the case of religion, it seems to be born out that something that does not exist cannot be disproved.

The arrogance of some churches should be questioned. The campaign to proselytize the world comes to mind. No matter what the culture or the custom elsewhere, Christians have assumed superiority for their belief in Christ, and, on that account, have set out to persuade other cultures to give up their convictions and take up the cross. This practice continues to this day. Pope John Paul II, on a trip to Mexico in 1999, warned his audience to beware of those newer, popular evangelists, and not to listen and give up their Catholicism. Yet, all are preaching a love of Christ being necessary for salvation.

Billy Graham, for example, openly declared his intention of evangelizing the world.[1] To presume superiority of one faith over another, especially when no evidence supports either faith, is a bit make-work in style.

Another example of theistic arrogance of some churches arises from two suppositions that seem to have been formulated from thin air. The first is that all persons are sinners, and the second is that if the sins are not expunged, the individuals will spend an eternity in hell. Freedom from guilt is achieved, of course, by accepting Christ in your heart. The advocates of theism thus feel justified in preaching that a lifetime in the fires of hell awaits those who fail to believe in Jesus Christ. Those clergy who have broken away from this premise have found themselves out of favor with their churches. Love of self seems a no-no. Many who understand this have soundly criticized even popular clergy like Billy Graham for terrorizing children with the fear of hell. Is arrogance at the base of such teaching? It seems so.

With theism being a belief in something supernatural, disavowing anything supernatural would define an a-theist. The word itself says non-Christian, and it comes off as a pejorative term. In a newspaper letter to the editor, for example, it was said that any person who is not a good practicing Christian, cannot be a good American.[2] One worries about that writer's attitude toward his/her Jewish or Islamic neighbors. It might be pointed out, however, that the many Chinese and Russians, raised under communist governments, were for generations without any faith in a supernatural Being. Many are atheists, and they collectively make up a substantial part of the world's population. Is applying a pejorative term to the millions upon millions of human beings who don't believe in Jesus Christ, or practice Judaism, morally healthy for those who do?

It should also be pointed out that the word atheist tells what a person is not, but not what a person is. For example, an individual who worships the moon could be an atheist, but so could a Buddhist. Thus, to be called an atheist does not specify what the belief of the person is. Atheism can be a valid and respectable way of looking at things. It can be clean and wholesome; it does not necessarily depend on miracles; it does not necessarily rely on unevidenced postulates; and it does not have to threaten purgatory for nonbelievers.

One might ask: What is wrong with believing in God, and in a hereafter, and in Jesus Christ as Lord, or whatever one's religion holds, if one were not to judge those who believe otherwise? The answer is that evidence and fact are useful, while myth, or emotionally holding to a belief, is not because concentration on myth takes the place of concentration on what is real. The problems of the world are real, and to think that such problems can be solved by praying to sacred myths is deceptive and takes away from doing real work.

Many people have received Christmas cards from Jerry Falwell asking for money, and declaring that, "...earnest, effective prayer is the only hope for our families, our nation, and our world." Billy Graham has done the same thing. He proposed a national day of prayer beseeching God's help in finding a solution to the Korean war.[3] Such advice is blind to the reality that solutions take thought and action. So we're back to comfort, compassion, and solace being as available without theism as with it. Righting wrongs takes real work, and everyone is capable of goodness and moral behavior if that behavior is what's taught and honored by society.

Another question that might be asked is: What is so seriously wrong with Christianity if spiritually, a belief in God and Christ's connection to God, have given so many a reason to exist for so long? The answer would need a little review of some facts.

At some ill-defined time, perhaps 6,000 to 4,000 years ago, thoughtful men realized that rules of conduct for communal living would be needed. They considered various rules, tossed them about, gradually refined them, and eventually produced the Ten Commandments. In order to give them credibility, they attributed them to God, and claimed they were handed down from God to Moses. That was the foundation of the Old Testament. They could be viewed as fabrications of human minds because there has never been any evidence to indicate otherwise. Moses was clearly disturbed with the direction of society as he saw it, and did separate himself to meditate to find an answer. That is the only evidenced fact.

In modern times (1830), another religious leader repeated this experience. His name was Joseph Smith, and he went up into the hills where he claimed to have received a golden tablet from God on which was written the *Book of Mormon* for the Mormon Church. Again, it was his word. Both Moses and Joseph Smith were strong minded men. Both were leader types. Both enjoyed power, and both were accepted as having received a message from a supernatural source.

After the Old Testament, Jesus was born, and his work on earth was to provide moral guidance. He was elevated eventually to live as a supernatural Being, and his connection with God was subsequently established by the Nicene Creed. That was according to an agreement made by mortals. Now the setting was laid. The public wanted to believe in a God, churches claimed that God was real, and there was no movement to refute the claim of the churches. Thus, a myth became an act of faith. A myth became a fact.

Various churches promoted this "fact" unendingly, with men eventually establishing Catholicism following Christ's death, and various clergy and leaders, thereafter, forming offshoots, such as the Episcopalian, Lutheran, and Calvinist churches, to name a few. But the history behind the foundation shows only evidence of men teaching, writing, and re-writing stories and rules which constitute faiths.

Now we come to the problem today. The central fault is that religious leaders like Billy Graham, Jerry Falwell, and Pat Robertson have taken the words of the Bible to be literally true. Having done that, and knowing that none can refute the words of the Bible, they sally forth disseminating propositions that they insist are true: all individuals are sinners, sin can be absolved only by accepting Christ as personal savior, and failure to accept Jesus Christ will condemn the individual to an eternity in the fires of hell. They offer their word as evidence, nothing else. It seems the central fault of Christianity is the acceptance of the Bible as a literal truth which allows the myths of faith to be broadcast as having a true and factual basis.

The Bible is considered well written, beautifully written even, but then we do have proof that scholarly men, who were supported by the churches, re-wrote it by hand for hundreds of years. There is no original to be seen. People travel to Trinity College in Dublin, Ireland, to view the Book of Kells, an illuminated manuscript of Gospels, because of its historic background and beauty. Jesus has red hair in Ireland, blond in Germany, and brown in Italy, and in paintings that were commissioned by the Vatican. He had none of this considering his birthplace and parents.

The Book of Common Prayer was written by Crammer in 1549, with variations since. Man created those prayers and the services that make up a Christian sect. These are the only types of facts that exist in religious history. Good men, meaning well, most wanting to help civilization, some wanting power and leadership positions, all created religions as we know them. That's why Christianity is a faith. Moses was adamant that God chose him to lead the Jews, and squelched the word of all others who tried to question this, as strong world leaders have been want to do. Peter did the same in establishing Catholicism. Judaism is a faith, as is Buddhism, and Islam. That's why the Christian churches have to keep up this incessant pleading that Christ be accepted as one's personal savior. If that pleading were to stop, the idea would evaporate because no evidence would prompt its renewal.

The Bible asserts the divinity of Christ and the existence of God. These assertions are supported only by symbolic stories and metaphors. Therefore, neither assertion is necessarily true. The churches' leaders, nevertheless, then turn around and threaten dreadful penalty if the assertions are not believed. When studied, it's obvious that the assertions are artificial because they stray from the historical words left by a man named Jesus. What he proclaimed was the evil of greed, the necessity of peace, and the acceptance of all humans as equals. The divinity of Christ is artificial, his message remains solid.

There are always scholars and theologians working on what is referred to here as myth, trying to find historical facts to substantiate beliefs of faith. However, when the truth people seek violates the physical laws of nature, it is not likely that validating evidence will be found. At the moment, churches distance themselves quite firmly from all miracle sightings or events. People of varying intelligence and education do connect to inner feelings of spirituality, but no organized religion holds license over those feelings. We must understand that no religion is higher than truth, and there is no truth without evidence.

There is also the situation of the agnostics. The agnostics don't know whether there's a God or not, so they remain uncommitted. If there is no God, they haven't claimed there is; and, if there is a God, they haven't claimed there isn't. It is a point of view that requires no faith or fact. It's not expected that more information on the presence or absence of God will come to them. The question has to be faced with the information now at hand. It can be seen that the agnostic makes no contribution to the discussion.

· · · · ·

CHAPTER 6 REFERENCES

1. Martin, W. *A Prophet with Honor. The Billy Graham Story*, William Morrow and Company, New York, 1991, p. 186.

2. *News-Press.* Ft. Myers, FL, Dec. 27, 1998, p. 16A.

3. Martin, W. Ibid., p. 131.

7

All religions have Gods.

Alternative Beliefs

WHILE CHRISTIANITY IS IN DOUBT because it relies on miracles and myths, it could be asked if there is any spiritually based philosophy with merit. According to encyclopedia information, there are only six main religions. Arranged according to approximate numbers of followers, these are:

> The six main religions and the number of followers:
> 1. Christianity 1,600,000,000
> 2. Islam 1,014,000,000
> 3. Hinduism 750,000,000
> 4. Buddhism 335,000,000
> 5. Confucianism 140,000,000
> 6. Judaism 13,000,000

To get an idea of their nature, it is advisable to take these up in chronological order. (Fig. F)

Hinduism

Possibly the earliest of all the main religions, Hinduism began thousands of years ago with a song that was sung by Indian sages. It had 1,500 stanzas and was known as the Rig Veda. The religion that evolved from this song differs clearly from Western concepts. Instead of a past, present, and future, Hinduism portrays time as standing still with only fluctuations that come and go. Rather than a flowing river with a source and destination, Hindu thought likens time to a lake that is motionless except for ripples that now and then roughen the surface. From this springs the idea that humans also come and go. Thus, after a brief life, the individual returns in some other form; that is, he or she is reincarnated.

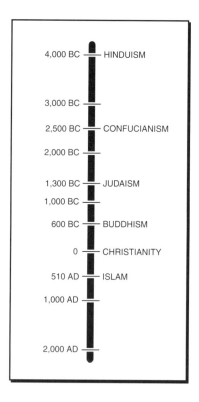

Fig. F. Chronological order of the main religions.

What a person returns as depends on his/her record from the preceding life. That record is known as a person's karma. While the earth is seen as having no purpose, the objective of the individual is to become one with God and thus escape the endless rounds of reincarnation. To become one with God (Nirvana) requires a life of self-discipline, purity, truth, detachment, charity, nonviolence, and compassion for all creatures.

Hinduism also has a supernatural world which brims with millions of types of gods. The main god, however, is Brahman, and the major gods below Brahman are Brahma the Creator, Vishnu the Preserver, and Shiva the Destroyer. Shiva gets rid of the old, and Vishnu returns with the next generation. Behavior in the past life or karma, determines the status of the individual in the next life. Thus exists the caste system in which the highest is the priestly class or Brahmins, and the lowest is the laborer/servant class or Sudras. There are intervening castes, and some have no caste at all and are known as Outcastes. Tradition mandates that the Outcastes neither be touched nor included in social activities. Such discrimination is presently prohibited by law.

Hinduism has admirable goals, the improvement of karma with each reincarnation, ultimately achieving a 'oneness with God' or Nirvana. The concept of time standing still, with only endless repetitions of human events, is fascinating. Reincarnation, the caste system, and the idea of major and minor gods is imaginary. They are mythical concepts, and instead of taking control of their own destiny, Hindus are resigned to letting fate take its own course, and then ascribing various events to forces beyond their control.

Confucianism

Confucius lived from 551 to 479 B.C.[1] He was the sage of ancient China, and its greatest philosopher. He was so revered that a temple to him is found in each of China's 2,000 counties.

His life was spent as a teacher, and his message was registered in the Four Books which were for the primary level of schooling, and the Five Classics which were for the secondary level. He believed in the dignity and native integrity, as well as the equality and educability, of all men.

At the center of this system of Confucius was humanity, representing love, benevolence, and manhood or human-relatedness. He believed that the greatness of man was measured by the extent of his humanity. This spirit was so central in his teaching that it was the philosophy of Confucius. The Golden Rule of Confucius was "Do not do unto others what one does not wish to be done unto." Confucius emphasized the kinship of all men, and the importance of expressing goodwill toward one another.

Confucius was not the founder of a religion in the usual sense. He believed in a universal moral force which he spoke of as heaven, although he spoke very little about traditional religion. He did regard much of formal religion as superstition, but he found much esthetic enjoyment in religious ritual. About heaven, he was prone to ask, "Does heaven speak?" He made no claim to his own divinity, and he made no reference to the supernatural.

If there is such a thing as an eternal verity, the Chinese have found it in the teachings of Confucius. It is idealistic humanism. For centuries Korea, Japan, the Ryukyus, and Vietnam have adopted Confucius as their sage and teacher. The teaching of Confucius is especially attractive because it shuns the supernatural, emphasizes love and goodwill, and promotes the sanctity of life. Small wonder that it has been so popular and so enduring.

Judaism

The formal Jewish religion began with Moses who lived between 1350 and 1250 B.C.[2] He founded the Hebrew nation and was its greatest prophet and central figure.

The Jewish faith has three characteristics. The most important is that it was the first religion to recognize only one God. That belief was later adopted by Christianity and Islam. The second characteristic is that Judaism has no central authority; each community has its own rabbi who is its spiritual leader and manages its communal affairs. The third characteristic is that it asks none to join the faith, and it is a religion for only one people, the Jews. And who is a Jew? Anyone whose mother or father is a Jew, and who has committed himself/herself to the rules of Judaism. Traditionally, the historical Jewish connection is traced through the mother's bloodline. Converts must apply; they are not solicited, and they must have valid spiritual reasons.

Moses climbed Mt. Sinai where God gave him two stone tablets on which were inscribed the Ten Commandments. He stayed on the mountain for 40 days and nights where, it is said, he neither ate nor drank. On his return, he found his people worshipping an idol, a golden calf. This enraged Moses and he smashed the tablets. God then told him to return to the mountain, which he did for another 40 days and nights, and this time God gave him another copy of the Ten Commandments, again engraved on two stone tablets. In addition, under God's direction, it is said, Moses wrote the first five books of the Hebrew Bible or Pentateuch. These five books made up the *Torah of Moses*.

The Torah teaches that there is only one God, and that He wants his followers to do what is just and merciful. He wants the faithful to understand that all people are created in the image of God and they deserve to be treated with dignity and respect.[3] The Torah is the will of God, and it describes the history of the Jews up to the death of Moses. It and the Talmud are the two sacred writings of Judaism. The Torah also makes up the first five books of the Christian Bible.

Today there are about 20 million Jews the world over, with roughly half in North America, and one quarter in each of Israel and in Europe/Russia.

In the years after the death of Moses, the Jews built a temple in Jerusalem. It was destroyed by the Babylonians in 586 B.C., and was rebuilt and then destroyed again by the Romans in 70 A.D. The Jews thus have a historical claim to a part of Jerusalem.

Moses died at age 120. He had been admired, and was known for the Exodus or leading the Jews out of Egypt, for leading his clan in the desert for 40 years, while they were rejected elsewhere, and for relocating them finally in the TransJordan region. Moses is the central figure of Jewish history. With all due respect, however, it must be realized that the supernatural is more myth than fact. That fact does not displace the rabbi from his position of leadership in an organization that enjoys social warmth, common understanding, and higher moral values.

Buddhism

In Nepal in the sixth century before Christ, a child was born who was to become founder of one of the world's great religions. His name was Siddartha Gautama, and he was a prince who lived in a palace. Although forbidden to leave the palace, he secretly journeyed out to see the plight of the common folk. He saw poverty and sickness and death all about. He wanted to alleviate the suffering, so at age 29 he left the palace in the dead of night after bidding his sleeping wife and infant son a silent good-bye. He dressed himself in the yellow robes of a mendicant monk and joined five holy men who advised him to starve himself. He did and it didn't help anyone. So he left them.

One day he wandered into a small village named Gaya and sat under a shady Bo tree, also called a Bodhi tree. He meditated for 49 days, and ate only enough to prevent hunger from consuming his thoughts. It was here that enlightenment came to him; he had found the answer to the riddle of life. Thereafter, he was known as Gautama Buddha. Buddha means enlightened one.

Buddha then traveled to Benares where he met his five companions, and where, in a park outside the city, he gave his first sermon on the meaning of life. He made two great pronouncements; the Four Noble Truths, and the Noble Eightfold Path. The four noble truths were that suffering was universal; the cause of suffering was craving; the cure for suffering was to eliminate craving; and, the craving was eliminated by following the eightfold path.

The Noble Eightfold Path included right knowledge, right interest, right speech, right conduct, right livelihood, right effort, right mindfulness, and right concentration. By following these instructions, man would pass on to Nirvana which was the goal of all earthly strivings.

Gautama Buddha had been a Hindu so it was natural for him to approve of the concepts of karma, reincarnation, and Nirvana. However, he did not approve of elaborate rituals, the caste system, or the idea that men had different spiritual potentials. The high ideals of Buddhism were widely accepted; i.e., tolerance, nonviolence, respect for individuals, the love of animals and the love of nature. These messages spread widely over India, China, Japan, Indonesia, Tibet, Pakistan, Afghanistan, Mongolia, Korea and more recently in the United States, or at least versions of this. The great virtue of Buddhism remains its selfless devotion to others.

One branch of Buddhism has a faint association with God and a hereafter, but the faith otherwise is devoid of such a connection. For that reason it is different from those faiths that rely mainly on divinities and a heaven. However, walking about in yellow robes with dishes for alms and food hand-outs, and offering prayers to statues of Buddha, including in the temple settings, are not unlike the worship of supernatural beings of other faiths.

Christianity

Christianity began with Jesus, who taught for not more than four years. His message was timeless: love, goodwill, mercy, justice, forgiveness, and humility. He had 12 disciples or Apostles, who carried his message throughout the Roman Empire. Jesus was thought to be king of the Jews. This worried the Romans, who thought he might lead a Jewish revolt against them, so they had him killed by crucifixion. He was only in early middle age, 33.

Much of Christ's teaching was done by the two Apostles, St. Peter and St. Paul. They claimed to have seen Jesus alive, after his death on the cross, giving rise to the Resurrection theory, one of the basic doctrines of the Christian faith. Both Apostles were later beheaded in Rome. The Romans, who worshipped idols, persecuted the Christians unmercifully until 380 A.D., when the Emperor Constantine made Christianity the official religion of the Empire. The Christian church taught the Old Testament, and assembled writings, especially the letters of St. Paul, to form the New Testament. Christianity spread widely.

Christianity remained one great community until the 800s when the church at Istanbul broke away from the church at Rome. The final separation in 1054 resulted in the Greek Catholic Church and the Roman Catholic Church. In the Middle Ages, 1100 to 1300, the Moslems invaded the Holy Land, which set off the Crusades. Then in the 1500s, large groups broke away from the Roman Catholics in the Protestant Reformation. Later, these Protestants segregated into various sects and denominations including the Lutherans, Methodists, Episcopalians, Baptists, Congregationalists, and Mormons.

Today, Christianity is the largest of the main religions. The main divisions of the Christian church are the Roman Catholic Church, the Protestant denominations, and the Greek Orthodox church. In approximate numbers, six of every ten Christians are Roman Catholic, just over two are Protestant, and one of every ten is Greek Orthodox. Christianity has influenced government, group and individual thought, and art for almost 2,000 years.[5]

While Christ's moral strictures are eternally true, they should be revered for themselves without any connection to myths. It is the Apostles who claim to have witnessed the resurrection, and it is the Nicene Creed that posits the oneness of man, Christ, and God. That creed is an arrangement made by mortals. Out of this welter of stories, fabricated by men, comes the stance of the church which today insists on the reality of Christ's divinity, and the reality of God's existence. The goodness and the necessity of the Christian morals are vouched for by myths that the church insists are truths. It is a false spirituality, and it blemishes the morals that Jesus taught and which need no crutch. The morals of Jesus, and the myths of the faith, are permanently independent from one another.

Islam

Islam is the youngest of the major religions of the world.[6] It is growing rapidly, and especially in America. The founder of Islam was Mohammed who was born in Mecca, Arabia, in 570, A.D. His youth was not especially remarkable, but in early adulthood he began reciting rhythmic prose. It came to him involuntarily and was presumed to be sent to him by Allah. Mohammed thus took himself to be the spokesman for God. For this faith, God was the one, the only, and the greatest God, superseding all others. What Mohammed spoke for was submission to Allah (Islam means submission), and what he recited became the sayings of the Koran.

These sayings acknowledge the hereafter, speaking of both the Gardens of Paradise and the terrors of hell, but concentrating mainly on directions for living in this world. They include honoring one's parents, helping the poor, protecting the orphans, being honorable in all dealings, avoiding drink, pork, and gambling, and always being humble before Allah. He spoke against the worship of idols, which offended many; and, on this account, he had to flee to Medina. That move was known as the Hegira or flight.

In 630 he returned to Mecca and proclaimed the Kaaba or cube, to be the sanctuary of Allah. It is now the most holy place in the Islamic world. Devout Moslems must attempt a pilgrimage to Mecca (Hadj) once in their lifetime. They pray, encircle the Kaaba seven times, and observe other rituals.

Mohammed proclaimed the "Five Pillars of Islam." The first was faith in Allah; whoever declares, "There is no God but Allah; Mohammed is his messenger," was a Moslem. They believed that the Christian Triune (Jesus, God, and the Holy Ghost) was polytheistic. The second was prayer repeated five times per day, always by kneeling, facing Mecca, and touching the head to the floor. The third was almsgiving for the support of the mosque and the poor.

The fourth was keeping the fast of Ramadan. In the ninth month of the year, Mohammed received his first revelation from Allah. This month (September) was set aside each year for fasting from dawn to dusk, continuing for the entire month. Each day, however, when the gun of sunset sounded, feasting began and presents were exchanged. The fifth pillar was the annual pilgrimage to Mecca.

Mohammed died in 632 A.D. Those who followed led successful military campaigns which brought Islamic control over Syria, Iraq, Palestine, Egypt, and the entire Persian Empire. These conquests took place between 635 and 650 A.D. The rampage took them to India on the east, the Atlantic on the west, and across the Straight of Gibraltar into Spain, Portugal, and France. It was the Battle of Tours in France in 732 that halted the advance and saved Europe for Christianity.

Since then the faithful have continued to multiply in numbers, and Islam is presently the second largest religious denomination on earth.

There is a haunting similarity between Mohammed being the spokesman for Allah, Jesus being the spokesman for God, and Oral Roberts healing through the sensations that God placed in his right arm. For that matter, Robert Schuller, Pat Robertson, and Jerry Falwell all lean toward their assertions as having come directly from God. Even Billy Graham, paragon of virtue and sincerity, asserts that if you will come forward and accept Christ, he will guarantee everlasting happiness in heaven. All of these sages speak with invisible credentials, and their promises are beyond refutation.

It is now evident that all of the main religions of the world are, to one degree or another, dependent on a deity. The least so dependent is Confucianism, although Confucius did speak of heaven. A main religion without a deity has yet to emerge.

♦ ♦ ♦ ♦ ♦

CHAPTER 7 REFERENCES

1. Mei, Y.P. "Confucius." *Encyclopedia Americana.* 7: 540, 1998.
2. Smith, J.Z., Editor. *HarperCollins Dictionary of Religion.* HarperCollins, Publishers, Inc., San Francisco, 1995, p. 598.
3. "Religion." *World Book Encyclopedia.* 11:179, 1995.
4. Smith, J.Z., Editor. Ibid., p. 599.
5. "Islam." *World Book Encyclopedia.* 3:406, 1960.
6. Smith, J.Z., Editor. Ibid., p. 498.

8

*Secular Humanism is the alternative
to myths formulated by their promoters
to suit their own needs.*

The Choice

LOOKING FOR A BELIEF SYSTEM that does not depend on a supernatural being, that does not have a pejorative or negative name, and that does not depend on miracles, guilt, or flights of fancy such as heaven, or hell or other idolatries of the mind that have nothing to do with reality, seems like a challenge; but, there are actually two belief systems that meet most of these requirements.

The first is the Unitarian persuasion. It was formed in the 1600s and later joined with a similar belief known as Universalism. The two formed one conjoined system that operates under separate management and is known as the Unitarian/Universalist Association or U/Us.

If anyone indicates an interest, the Unitarians will give them a card that tells what they believe in. They list nine separate convictions.[1] Four of them seem above question for any mindset.

The first of these states, "We believe in the never ending search for Truth. If the mind and heart are truly free and open, the revelations which appear to the human spirit are infinitely numerous, eternally fruitful, and wondrously exciting." To avoid being picayune, we shall not question the word spirit. This fits the requirements. The second states, "We believe in the worth and dignity of each human being. All people on earth have an equal claim to life, liberty, and justice and no idea, ideal, or philosophy is superior to a single human life." Also faultless for the requirements.

The third states, "We believe in the motive force of love. The governing principle in human relationships is the principle of love, which always seeks the welfare of others and never seeks to hurt or destroy." This is practically an endorsement of nonviolence. The last of the unchallengeable convictions states, "We believe in the necessity of the democratic process. Records are open to scrutiny, elections are open to members, and ideas are open to criticism so that people might govern themselves." These four of the nine convictions are fine for the search.

Of the two convictions that do not fit the criteria of the search, the first is, "We believe in the authority of reason and conscience. The ultimate arbiter of religion is not a church, or a document, or an official, but the personal choice and decision of the individual." The problem here is that one dictionary defines the word religion as belief in a supernatural being. The statement thus allows some or all to believe in a God, and that conflicts with the purpose of finding a belief that is devoid of such an idea.

The second says, "We believe in the unity of experience." The meaning of this sentence is obscure. It goes on, "There is no fundamental conflict between faith and knowledge, religion and the world, and the sacred and the secular, since they all have their source in the same reality." There is a fundamental conflict between faith and knowledge, and between the sacred and the secular. Moreover, "having their source in the same reality," is unclear.

Finally, three of the Unitarian convictions are seriously in question when set against the purpose of finding a nontheistic belief system. One begins, "We believe in the freedom of religious expression." Considering the meaning of the word religion, this principle precludes a nontheistic belief. Another says, "We believe in the toleration of religious ideas." The same criticism applies. The third is also subject to the same criticism, since it begins with, "We believe in the ethical application of religion." All three conflict with a nontheistic belief system and for this reason the Unitarian convictions do not fulfill the objectives of the search.

There is another choice. It's called Secular Humanism. It shuns theism, and is a term that is neither pejorative nor negative. Secular Humanisn has an indefinite beginning, going back perhaps hundreds of years, but the first formal expression was the Humanist Manifesto I, published in 1933. It began with these words, "The time has come for widespread recognition of the radical changes in religious beliefs throughout the modern world. The time is past for mere revision of traditional attitudes. Science and economic change have disrupted the old beliefs. Religions the world over are under the necessity of coming to terms with new conditions created by vastly increased knowledge and experience. In every field of human activity, the vital movement is now in the direction of candid and explicit humanism."[2] The tract cites 17 principles.

In 1973, that first expression of purpose was amended as the Human Manifesto II. The Preface included the following paragraph: "As in 1933, humanists still believe that traditional theism, especially faith in the prayer-hearing God, assumed to love and care for persons, to hear and understand their prayers, and to be able to do something about them, is an unproved and outmoded faith. Salvationism, based on mere affirmation, still appears as harmful, diverting people with false hopes of heaven hereafter. Reasonable minds look to other means for survival."[3] After the Preface, 17 principles were cited under five headings.

Secular Humanism: The 17 Principles in their Entirety

Religion

First: We find insufficient evidence for the belief in the existence of a supernatural; it is either meaningless or irrelevant to the question of the survival and fulfillment of the human race. As nontheists, we begin with humans not God, nature not deity. But we can discover no divine purpose or providence for the human species. While there is much that we do not know, humans are responsible for what we are or will become. And no deity will save us; we must save ourselves.

Second: Promises of immortal salvation or fear of eternal damnation are both illusory and harmful. They distract humans from present concerns, from self actualization, and from rectifying social injustices. Modern science discredits such historic concepts as the "ghost in the machine" and the "separable soul." Rather, science affirms that the human species is an emergence from natural evolutionary forces. As far as we know, the total personality is a function of the biologic organism transacting in a social and cultural context. There is no credible evidence that life survives the death of the body. We continue to exist in our progeny and in the way that our lives have influenced others in our culture.

Ethics

Third: Ethics is autonomous and situational, needing no theological or ideological sanction.

Fourth: Reason and intelligence are the most effective instruments that humankind possesses. There is no other substitute: neither faith nor passion suffices in itself. The controlled use of scientific methods, which have transformed the natural and social sciences since the Renaissance, must be extended further in the solution of human problems.

The Individual

Fifth: The precariousness and dignity of the individual person is a central humanist value. We believe in maximum individual autonomy consonant with social responsibility.

Sixth: In the area of sexuality, we believe that intolerant attitudes, often cultivated by orthodox religions and puritanical cultures, unduly repress sexual conduct. The right to birth control, abortion, and divorce should be recognized. While we do not approve of exploitive, denigrating forms of sexual expression, neither do we wish to prohibit, by law or social sanction, sexual behavior between consenting adults. The many varieties of sexual exploration should not in themselves be considered "evil." Without countenancing mindless permissiveness or unbridled promiscuity, a civilized society should be a tolerant one. Short of harming others or compelling them to do likewise, individuals should be permitted to express their sexual proclivities and pursue their life-styles as they desire. We wish to cultivate the development of a responsible attitude toward sexuality, in which humans are not exploited as sexual objects, and in which intimacy, sensitivity, respect, and honesty in interpersonal relations are encouraged. Moral education for children and adults is an important way of developing awareness and sexual maturity.

Democratic Society

Seventh: To enhance freedom and dignity the individual must experience a full range of civil liberties in all societies. This includes freedom of speech and the press, political democracy, the legal right of opposition to governmental policies, fair judicial process, religious liberty, freedom of association, and artistic, scientific, and culture freedom. It also includes a recognition of an individual's right to die with dignity, euthanasia, and the right to suicide. We oppose the increasing invasion of privacy, by whatever means, in both totalitarian and democratic societies.

Eighth: Decision making must be decentralized to include widespread involvement of people at all levels – social, political, and economic.

Ninth: The separation of church and state and the separation of ideology and state are imperatives. The state should encourage maximum freedom for different moral, political, religious, and social values in society. It should not favor any particular religious bodies through the use of public monies, nor espouse a single ideology and function, thereby, as an instrument of propaganda or oppression, particularly against dissenters.

Tenth: Humane societies should evaluate economic systems, not by rhetoric or ideology, but by whether or not they increase economic well-being for all individuals and groups, minimize poverty and hardship, increase the sum of human satisfaction, and enhance the quality of life.

Eleventh: The principle of moral equality must be furthered through elimination of all discrimination based upon race, religion, sex, age, or national origin. This means the equality of opportunity and recognition of talent and merit. Individuals should be encouraged to contribute to their own betterment. If unable, then society should provide means to satisfy their basic economic health, and cultural needs, including, wherever resources make possible, a minimum guaranteed annual income. We are concerned for the welfare of the aged, the infirm, the disadvantaged, and also for the outcasts – the mentally retarded, abandoned, or abused children, the handicapped, prisoners, and addicts - for all who are neglected or ignored by society.

We believe in the right to universal education. Everyone has the right to the cultural opportunity to fulfill his or her unique capacities and talents. The schools should foster satisfying and productive living. They should be open at all levels to any and all; the achievement of excellence should be encouraged. Innovative and experimental forms of education are to be welcomed.

World Community

Twelfth: We deplore the division of humankind on nationalistic grounds. We have reached a turning point in human history where the best option is to transcend the limits of national sovereignty and to move toward the building of a world community in which all sectors of the human family can participate. Thus we look to the development of a system of world law and a world order based upon transitional federal government.

Thirteenth: The world community must renounce the resort to violence and force as a method of solving international disputes. We believe in the peaceful adjudication of difference by international courts and by the development of the arts of negotiation and compromise. War is obsolete. So is the use of nuclear, biological, and chemical weapons. It is a planetary imperative to reduce the level of military expenditures and turn these savings to peaceful and people-oriented uses.

Fourteenth: The world community must engage in cooperative planning concerning the use of rapidly depleting resources. The planet earth must be considered a single ecosystem. Ecological damage, resource depletion, and excessive population growth must be checked by international concord.

Fifteenth: World poverty must cease. Hence extreme disproportion in wealth, income, and economic growth should be reduced on a worldwide basis.

Sixteenth: Technology is a vital key to human progress and development. We deplore any neoromantic efforts to condemn indiscriminately all technology and science or to counsel retreat from its further extension and use for the good of humankind. We would resist any moves to censor basic scientific research on moral, political, or social grounds.

Seventeenth: We must expand communication and transportation across frontiers. Travel restrictions must cease. The world must be open to diverse political, ideological, and moral viewpoints and evolve a worldwide system of television and radio information and education. We thus call for full international cooperation in culture, science, the arts, and technology across ideological borders. We must learn to live openly together or we shall perish together.

That completes the seventeen principles of the Humanist Manifesto II. There are two more notes in closing. "We urge recognition of the common humanity of all people. We further urge the use of reason and compassion to produce the kind of world we want – a world in which peace, prosperity, freedom, and happiness are widely shared. Let us not abandon that vision in despair or cowardice. We are responsible for what we are or will be. Let us work together for a humane world by means commensurate with humane ends.

"At the present juncture of history, commitment to all humankind is the highest commitment of which we are capable; it transcends the narrow allegiances of church, state, party, class, or race in moving toward a wider vision of human potentiality. What more daring a goal for humankind than for each person to become, in ideal as well as practice, a citizen of the world community."[4]

These are inspiring words! These are lofty goals! It should be understood that Secular Humanism has been embraced by Kurt Vonnegut (Honorary President), Carl Sagan, Lester R. Brown, Margaret Atwood, Betty Friedan, Gloria Steinem, 'Maggie' Kuhn, John Kenneth Galbraith, Gene Roddenberry, Stephen Jay Gould, Donald C. Johanson, E.O. Wilson, Jonas Salk, Fay Wattleton, and Bill Baird. Earlier there were also Isaac Asimov, Andrei Sakharov, R. Buckminster Fuller, Erich Fromm, A Philip Randolph, Margaret Sanger, John Dewey, Bertrand and Dora Russell, and Albert Einstein. Secular Humanism constitutes a cultural revolution.

It is, of course, anathema to the Evangelicals, partly because it rejects fundamental Christian creeds, and partly because the humanists have not consulted with the leaders of orthodox religions. To be bypassed without even consultation angers the Evangelicals. They have simply been ignored. The incensed Evangelicals believe that Secular Humanisn, or just Humanism, is the Godless principle that erodes the moral foundation of America. Much of their distress is directed toward the Supreme Court.

Pat Robertson, for example, contends that in matters of law, the Supreme Court, composed of non-elected officials, cannot have the last word. He has said that the people he deals with, the Evangelicals, despise the Supreme Court, that they feel that the Supreme Court has trampled on their schools, religious liberties, and their method of government in an egregious fashion.[5]

The influential conservative religious author, Tim LaHaye wrote that many of the evils in the world today could be traced to Humanism, which he feels has taken over the government, the U.N., education, TV, and most other influential things in life.[6] The extent of his conservative point of view is indicated by his attitude toward the statue of David by Michelangelo. LaHaye believes such glorification of the body is contrary to God's command that Adam and Eve wear skins, with man demanding the freedom to go naked ever since.[7]

The solution to the problem, according to the Evangelicals, is to report to the ballot box, vote the Humanists out, and restore the Bible-believers to their rightful place in civil matters. LaHaye has written that no Humanist is qualified to hold any governmental office in America – any position that requires him/her to think in the best interest of America. He has written his belief that the major problems of our day – moral, educational, economical, and governmental – are primarily caused by the fact that over 50 per cent of our legislators are either committed Humanists or are severely influenced in their thinking by false theories of Humanism.[8] This would be news to them, as over 50 per cent actually think of themselves as Christians, perhaps just not LaHaye's kind.

Regardless of such extreme views, Secular Humanism is the core of the emerging cultural revolution. It's a liberal drift that characterizes mainstream culture in the twentieth century, and has permeated its institutions. These include the public schools, the courts, television, movies, theater, and literature. Secular Humanism is the cultural wave of the future.

Thus, the lines are drawn. On the one side are those whose views are validated solely by a book written by many men, largely unknown, over a period of many years. Their beliefs conflict with the laws of nature, are devoid of objective evidence, and depend on such other-worldly ideas as heaven, hell, uniform guilt, resurrection, and, for some, the immaculate conception.

On the other side is the belief, dedicated to the improvement of individuals and society, that is disciplined by objective evidence, that rejects falsely assumed authority, that turns away from meaningless pageantry, and that rejects such idolatries of the mind as the resurrection and the uniformity of guilt. Secular Humanism sweeps away the haze of the past. To those who look closely, it is unblemished, positive, and prospective.

Secular Humanism will march steadfastly forward as more people who question the established myths and become dissatisfied with the intolerant teachings of organized religions discover its premise. It will also satisfy people's desire to support an approved principle and belong to a like-minded community.

♦ ♦ ♦ ♦ ♦

CHAPTER 8 REFERENCES

1. Unitarian/Universalist Association handout, 1999.
2. *The Humanist Manifesto I* and *II*. American Humanist Association, Amherst, NY, 1988.
3. Hadden, J.K., and Shupe, A. *Televangelism. Power and Politics on God's Frontier.* Henry Holt and Company, New York, 1988.
4. *The Humanist Manifesto I.* American Humanist Association, Amherst, NY, 1973.
5. Hadden, J.K., and Shupe, A. Ibid., p. 64.
6. Ibid., p. 69.
7. Ibid., p. 70.
8. Ibid., p. 72.

(Copies of *the Humanist Manifesto I and II* may be obtained from the American Humanist Association, 7 Harwood Drive, Post Office Box 1188, Amherst, New York 14226-7188)

PART THREE

Two reasons justify the challenge to Christianity. The first is that its substance is unproved. Mature, educated, and responsible adults cannot allow their lives to be dominated by myth. The second is that a more rational belief system is available. It is Secular Humanism, with its main advantage being that it replaces faith with objective truth. Also, Secular Humanism improves our understanding of many of the problems that face society, among them – church-state separation, homosexuality, equality of races, abortion, the treatment of prisoners, and war. These matters should be explored by people of all faiths, for it is evident that present solutions are not succeeding.

◆ ◆ ◆ ◆ ◆

9

*Government must not be
dominated by religious beliefs.*

Church-State Separation

IT MIGHT BE ASKED how the Secular Humanists pray when they don't have a deity. Without a supernatural body or even lesser gods, who will the Humanists revere, aspire to be like, and how will they improve society?

The Secular Humanists don't pray. That's another Christian practice that's man-made. We are unique, each of us, and we are the best that evolution has produced. It has taken four thousand six hundred million years for us to reach our present state. Accordingly, we have much to protect. The Humanist meetings therefore, discuss the problems of the day, and consider how we, by ourselves, may contend with them and solve them. The proceedings are founded in goodwill and mutual respect, and the realization that we must determine our own destiny because, so far as the evidence indicates, there is no one else to do it.

The meetings are not all that different from traditional church services. Cordiality and friendship prevail, love undergirds the whole concept, songs are sung, sometimes a choir contributes, and the importance of doing the best we can for each other is widely recognized. Much of the church music has been inspired by lofty ideals from classical to country to folk, and some rock. We bind together for the welfare of all rather than separate into artificial units that are often hostile to one another.

There are consequences if the switch to Humanism is not made. For example, with conservative or evangelical Christianity, we continue to believe in concepts which call upon prayer for one group to prevail over another. We may be asked to continue to consider creationism, which will obscure the understanding of evolution. We will be encouraged to believe that "effective prayer" is the only hope for our families, our nation, and our world.[1] We will be asked to believe that appeals to God can marshal public opinion to the support of war.[2] We will be asked to believe that prayer can affect the outcome of war.[3] We would continue to believe that human actions and historical events reflect God's divine plan, that the world is irredeemable, and that human salvation is predetermined by God.[4] We will be encouraged to believe that fate is affected by prayer.

Thus, conservative Christianity believes that ideas without evidence are true, and that fate is an outcome to be idly accepted rather than a challenge to be aggressively met. From the standpoint of progress, all of this is negative.

On the other hand, if we turn to Secular Humanism, all of the foregoing negatives are avoided. In addition, five areas beg for immediate attention. They are education, abortion, homosexuality, crime, and war.

Education requires attention because the Christian Coalition threatens to take over the state and Secular Humanism stands in the way. The conflict becomes emotional rather than intellectual. The separation of church and state thus becomes a critical issue. Some church leaders want to prohibit abortions while parts of the public disagree. The question needs resolution. Some churches reject homosexuality; that question also needs attention. Crime and war are both subject to considerations not presently conceived of by the Christian status quo. For these reasons all five are affected by Secular Humanism in a natural way.

Education

The critical question seems to be: Why is it necessary to keep the church and state separate? If Christian church thought gets into the affairs of state, it may come to dominate the state, and then the Christian religions control the state. Can we imagine, for example, America under the domination of the Christian Coalition, with Pat Robertson controlling policy?

This might be seen to be carrying the matter too far, but there is evidence in every election that this is the goal of some. The Christian Coalition has two powerful allies. One is the mighty effect of the Catholic and Protestant churches themselves, and the other is the powerful effect of television which reaches into millions of homes on weekends and somewhat fewer throughout the week. There is a chaplain who presides over the Legislature. Presidents must be seen as church-going. God's name is evoked when congressmen and senators, as well as their state equivalents, are fighting for the passage of a bill.

Ralph Reed, who used to be Pat Robertson's lieutenant, has said that Christians have to take back the country, one precinct at a time, one neighborhood at a time, and one state at a time. He has stated that he believes that in his lifetime he will see a country once again governed by Christians and Christian values.[5] That type of statement reveals the political aspiration of the Christian Coalition. It is the central problem; churches must not be allowed to control the affairs of state.

Tim LaHaye, the conservative religious activist, also urges the public, led by their ministers, to go to the polls and vote the Bible-believers back into power.[6]

An example of this political problem happened in Fort Myers, Florida. That city lies in the Bible belt of America. It's a community of 75,000 or so, and the school board has five members. In a recent election three of the five turned out to be members or supporters of the Christian Coalition. One of their first moves was to initiate a course on the study of the Protestant (King James) Bible in the public high schools. The community immediately rose up in opposition because this was exactly what Ralph Reed had urged, and it was seen to be exactly the mechanism by which the Christian church would indoctrinate the public and eventually take over the state.

Meetings were held, pamphlets were sent out, and speeches were made. In the same week, one public meeting was titled, "Saving Our Schools from the Religious Right," and the other was labeled, "Stop Anti-Christian Bigotry." It came down to an agreement that made it acceptable to teach a course on the Bible as history, but not to proselytize the students to become members of the Christian church. The course was an elective, it was not especially popular, and in the next election, two of the three Christian-pushing members of the school board were not re-elected.

We might question just how this political trend of churches can be stopped. After all, we have free speech in this country, and the Christian Coalition must be free to urge high school students to join the Christian church.

The answer, of course, is that they are, but not on public property. With taxes being paid by all of the public, the Hindus, Catholics, Buddhists, agnostics, atheists and others with particular religions should all have a share. It would not be fair for the tax revenue to be used for the teaching of Protestant Christian values while disregarding the others. So public property, supported by all of the people, cannot be used in this selective way. That fact, alone, should end the debate.

We might also guess that it would be more or less easy to teach a course on the Bible as history, and then slip in a little proselytizing for the Christian Coalition. For this reason, the government has set up elaborate guidelines about the limits of this kind of teaching. In 1995, President Clinton sent out some guidelines on the teaching of religion. The guidelines were titled, "Religion in the Public Schools: A Joint Statement of Current Law." It was signed by a broad spectrum of religious and philosophical groups.[7] The signers accepted a commitment to the freedom of religious practice on the one hand, and the separation of church and state on the other. The seriousness of the "Joint Statement" is indicated by its thoroughness. With the exception of minor deletions, the statement is recorded here in its entirety.

Religion in the Public Schools: A Joint Statement of Current Student Law

Student Prayers

Students have the right to pray individually or in groups to discuss their religious views with their peers so long as they are not disruptive. Because the Establishment Clause does not apply to purely private speech, students enjoy the right to read their Bibles or other scriptures, say grace before meals, pray before tests, and discuss religion with other willing student listeners.

In the classroom, students have the right to pray quietly, except when required to be actively engaged in school activities (Students may not decide to pray just as a teacher calls on them.). In informal settings, such as in the cafeteria or in the halls, students may pray either audibly or silently, subject to the same rules of order as apply to other speech in these locations. However, the right to engage in voluntary prayer does not include, for example, the right to have a captive audience listen or compel other students to participate.

Graduation Prayer and Baccalaureates

School officials may not mandate or organize prayer at graduation, nor may they organize a religious baccalaureate ceremony. If the school generally rents out its facilities to private groups, it must rent them out on the same terms, and on a first come, first served basis, to organizers of privately sponsored religious baccalaureate services, provided that the school does not extend preferential treatment to the baccalaureate ceremony and the school disclaims official endorsement of the program.

(The courts have reached conflicting conclusions under the federal Constitution on student initiated prayer at graduation. Until this issue is authoritatively resolved, schools should ask their lawyers what rules should apply.)

Official Participation or Encouragement of Religious Activity

Teachers and school administrators, when acting in those capacities, are representatives of the state, and, in those capacities, are themselves prohibited from encouraging or soliciting student religious or anti-religious activity. Similarly, when acting in their official capacities, teachers may not engage in religious activities with their students. However, teachers may engage in private religious activity in faculty lounges.

Teaching About Religion

Students may be taught about religion, but public schools may not teach religion. As the U.S. Supreme Court has repeatedly said, 'It might well be said that one's education is not complete without a study of comparative religion, or the history of religion and its relationship to the advancement of civilization.' It would be difficult to teach music, literature and most social studies without considering religious influences.

The history of religion, comparative religion, the Bible (or other scripture) as literature (either as a separate course or within some other existing course), are all permissible public school subjects. It is both permissible and desirable to teach objectively about the role of religion in the history of the United States and other countries. One can teach that the Pilgrims came to this country with a particular religious vision, that Catholics and others have been subject to persecution, or that many of those participating in the abolitionists women's suffrage and civil rights' movements had religious motivations.

These same rules apply to the recurring controversy surrounding theories of evolution. Schools may teach about explanations of life on earth, including religious ones (such as creationism) in comparative religion or social studies classes.

In science class, however, they may present only genuinely scientific critiques of, or evidence for, any explanation of life on earth, but not religious critiques (beliefs unverifiable by scientific methodology). Schools may not refuse to teach evolutionary theory in order to avoid giving offense to religion nor may they circumvent these rules by labeling as science an article of religious faith.

Public schools must not teach as scientific fact or theory any religious doctrine, including creationism, although any genuinely scientific evidence for or against any explanation of life may be taught. Just as they may neither advance nor inhibit any religious doctrine, teachers should not ridicule, for example, a student's religious explanation for life on earth.

Students may express their religious beliefs in the form of reports, homework and artwork, and such expressions are constitutionally protected. Teachers may not reject or correct such submissions simply because they include a religious symbol or address religious themes.

Likewise, teachers may not require students to modify, include or exclude religious views in their assignments, if germane. These assignments should be judged by ordinary academic standards of substance, relevance, appearance and grammar.

Somewhat more problematic from a legal point of view are other public expressions of religious views in the classroom. Unfortunately, for school officials, there are traps on either side of this issue, and it is possible that litigation will result no matter what course is taken.

It is easier to describe the settled cases than to state clear rules of law. Schools must carefully steer between the claims of student speakers who assert a right to express themselves on religious subjects and the asserted right of student listeners to be free of unwelcome religious persuasion in a public school classroom.

Religious or anti-religious remarks made in the ordinary course of classroom discussion or student presentations are permissible and constitute a protected right. If in a sex education class a student remarks that abortion should be illegal because God has not permitted it, a teacher should not silence the remark, ridicule it, rule it out of bounds or endorse it, any more than a teacher may silence a student's religious-based comment in favor of choice for abortion.

If a class assignment calls for an oral presentation on a subject of the student's choosing, and, for example, the student responds by conducting a religious service, the school has the right, as well as the duty, to prevent itself from being used as a church. Other students are not voluntarily in attendance and cannot be forced to become an unwilling congregation.

Teachers may rule out-of-order religious remarks that are irrelevant to the subject at hand. In a discussion of Hamlet's sanity, for example, a student may not interject a view on creationism.

Distribution of Religious Literature

Students have the right to distribute religious literature to their schoolmates, subject to those reasonable time, place, and manner or other constitutionally acceptable restrictions imposed on the distribution of all non-school literature. Thus, a school may confine distribution of all literature to a particular table at particular times. It may not single out religious literature for burdensome regulation.

Outsiders may not be given access to the classroom to distribute religious or anti-religious literature. No court has yet considered whether, if all other community groups are permitted to distribute literature in common areas of public schools, religious groups must be allowed to do so on equal terms subject to reasonable time, place and manner restrictions.

"See You at the Pole"
(Optional student prayers at a campus flagpole)
Student participation in before or after school events, such as "see you at the pole," is permissible. School officials, acting in an official capacity, may neither discourage nor encourage participation in such an event.

Religious Persuasion versus Religious Harassment
Students have the right to speak to, and attempt to persuade, their peers about religious topics just as they do with regard to political topics. But school officials should intercede to stop student religious speech if it turns into religious harassment aimed at a student or a small group of students.

While it is constitutionally permissible for a student to approach another and issue an invitation to attend church, repeated invitations in the face of a request to stop constitute harassment. Where this line is to be drawn in particular cases will depend on the age of the students and other circumstances.

Equal Access Act
Student religious clubs in secondary schools must be permitted to meet and to have equal access to campus media to announce their meetings, if a school receives federal funds and permits any student non-curricular club to meet during non-instructional time. This is the command of the Equal Access Act

A non-curricular club is any club not related directly to a subject taught or soon-to-be taught in the school. Although schools have the right to ban all non-curriculum clubs, they may not dodge the law's requirement by the expedient of declaring all clubs curriculum-related. On the other hand, teachers may not actively participate in club activities and "non-school persons" may not control or regularly attend club meetings.

The act's constitutionality has been upheld by the Supreme Court, rejecting claims that the act violates the Establishment clause. The act's requirements are described in more detail in "The Equal Access Act and the Public Schools: Questions and Answers on the Equal Access Act," a pamphlet published by a broad spectrum of religious and civil liberties groups.

Religious Holidays

Generally, public schools may teach about religious holidays, and may celebrate the secular aspects of the holiday and objectively teach about their religious aspects. They may not observe the holidays as religious events. Schools should generally excuse students who do not wish to participate in holiday events. Those interested in further details should see "Religious Holidays in the Public Schools: Questions and Answers," a pamphlet published by a broad spectrum of religious and civil liberties groups.

Excusal from Religiously Objectionable Lessons

Schools enjoy substantial discretion to excuse individual students from lessons which are objectionable to that student or to his or her parent on the basis of religion. Schools can exercise that authority in ways which would defuse many other conflicts over curriculum content. If it is proved that particular lessons substantially burden a student's free exercise of religion and if the school cannot prove a compelling interest in requiring attendance, the school would be legally required to excuse the student.

Teaching Values

Schools may teach civic virtues, including honesty, good citizenship, sportsmanship, courage, respect of the rights and freedoms of others, respect for persons and their property, civility, the dual virtues of moral conviction and tolerance.

Subject to whatever rights of excusal exist under the federal constitution and state law, schools may teach sexual abstinence and contraception; whether and how schools teach these sensitive subjects is a matter of educational policy. However, these may not be taught as religious tenets. The mere fact that most, if not all, religions also teach these values does not make it unlawful to teach them.

Religious messages on T-shirts and the like may not be singled out for suppression. Students may wear religious attire, such as yarmulkes and head scarves, and they may not be forced to wear gym clothes that they regard, on religious grounds, as immodest.

Released Time

Schools have the discretion to dismiss students to off-premises religious instruction, provided that schools do not encourage or discourage participation or penalize those who do not attend. Schools may not allow religious instruction by outsiders on the premises during the school day.

The government released its report. The comprehensiveness of it indicates the seriousness with which it takes the question of the separation of church and state. The former must never take control of the latter.

◆ ◆ ◆ ◆ ◆

CHAPTER 9 REFERENCES

1. Falwell, J. *Faith Partners.* January, 1998.
2. *News-Press.* Ft. Myers, FL, February 23, 1998.
3. Martin, W. *Prophet with Honor.* William Morrow and Company, Inc., New York, 1991, p. 151.
4. Lee, M. "Omega Watch in Cascade." *The Newsletter of the College of Arts and Sciences,* University of Oregon, Spring, 1998, p. 4.
5. Reed, R. *The Interfaith Alliance.* Washington, DC, Undated.
6. Hadden, J. K., and Shupe, A. *Televangelism. Power and Politics on God's Frontier.* Henry Holt and Company, 1998, p. 75.
7. "Reading, Writing and Religion," *News-Press.* Ft. Myers, FL, May 10, 1998.

10

*Saving fetuses while jeopardizing
women is morally questionable.*

Abortion

THE CATHOLIC CHURCH and certain conservative Protestant denominations have wanted to prohibit abortions, whereas, the secular society has voted to allow abortions. That difference has created one of the most divisive issues of our time. Secular Humanism suggests a new orientation to this question that may be helpful.

A brief review of pregnancy will help define the exact issue in medical terms. The human gestation period is nine months or 36 weeks. This period is separated into three trimesters of 12 weeks each. Fertilization begins when the sperm penetrates the ovum. This normally happens when the ovum (egg), having been expelled from the ovary, is in transit down the uterine tube. Fertilization produces the zygote. The zygote continues down the uterine tube, and three days after fertilization implants in the lining of the uterus (endometrium). The structures that develop in the endometrium are the fetus and the placenta. These are collectively known as the conceptus.

During the first 12 weeks, the developing structure is an embryo, and in the second and third trimesters it is the fetus. Fetal movement, or quickening, is felt by the mother at about five months of gestation.[1] Viability usually occurs after the sixth month of pregnancy, and is the time at which the baby can survive outside of the uterus. The age of gestation is calculated from the first day of the last menstrual period. The maternal mortality of pregnancy is about 8 per 100,000 live births.[2]

Abortion is the interruption of pregnancy. It may be spontaneous or induced. Spontaneous abortion, also known as miscarriage, occurs in about 25 per cent of pregnancies.[3] Ninety per cent of spontaneous abortions occur in the first trimester, and more often in women under 17 or over 35 years of age.[4] It also occurs more often in women who have had difficulty in becoming pregnant. While not all causes are known, many are due to non-inherited genetic defects, the most frequent of which is an abnormality of chromosomal number. This is due to a fault of cell division in the embryo which occurs just after fertilization. This does not increase the chance of another miscarriage in a subsequent pregnancy.

A less common cause of miscarriage is an inherited chromosomal defect. The defect may be visible by microscopic examination of the chromosomes in the cells from the fetus and the parents. From these findings, an estimate of the chance of a subsequent miscarriage from the same defect may often be made.

Induced abortion is the use of drugs or instruments to interrupt pregnancy. During the first trimester the most common method is suction curettage. A small-bore flexible tube is inserted through the undilated cervical canal into the endometrial cavity where suction removes the embryo and placenta. The drug RU-486, may also be used at the same time; it blocks the action of progesterone which normally prepares the uterus to receive and nourish the embryo.

In the second trimester a spoon-shaped knife is inserted through the dilated cervical canal into the endometrial cavity where the lining is scraped and the fetus and placenta are removed. The knife is a curette, and the procedure is known as a Dilatation and Curettage or D&C. Also, in this trimester prostaglandins or a salt solution may be injected into the amniotic sac that surrounds the fetus and causes the uterine muscles to contract and expel the fetus and placenta.

The maternal mortality from each of these procedures in the first and second trimesters, is about 3 per 100,000 abortions.[5] Late abortions in the third trimester utilize fluid injections into the amniotic sac, and surgical emptying of the uterus; both are attended by a higher maternal mortality than with first or second trimester abortions.

Abortion was widely approved of until the advent of Christianity, when society turned against the practice. At that time abortion was condemned only when it was performed after animation, which meant the instillation of the soul. Animation was said by church scholars to occur 40 days after conception.[6] This doctrine persisted until 1588 when it was abrogated by Pope Sixtus V, who proclaimed that the embryo is infused with a soul at the time of fertilization, and therefore, abortion at any time of pregnancy was a violation of the sanctity of life.

In 1869, Pope Pius IX condemned abortion from the moment of fertilization, and in 1895, the Roman Catholic church declared abortion never to be justifiable. This doctrine was asserted again in 1930 by Pope Pius XI. Today the Catholic church condemns all abortions except those in which fetal loss is incidental to a procedure necessary to save the woman's life. The Roman Catholic church is said to be the leading opponent of abortion.[7]

Before the mid-1800s, abortion was not a crime in the United States if it took place before quickening, the moment at which the mother feels fetal movement. Movement is usually felt around the fifth month of gestation.[8] The Catholic church and certain Protestant denominations urged against abortion; and, by

1900, all states except Kentucky had made abortion a serious crime. Opposition to this gradually developed, and by the early 1970s, 14 states permitted abortions if the mother's life were in danger, or if the pregnancy were caused by incest or rape.[9]

In 1973, only four states guaranteed a woman the right to choose for herself whether to terminate her pregnancy.[10] In the early 1970s, the political tide turned. Feminism arose, and women began to take leadership roles in business. Women also demanded control over their own lives, and they felt entitled to legal and safe abortions. Physicians took over the practice, and abortions were granted more or less freely.

Against this was the Catholic church and some Protestant denominations that regarded abortions as sinful. The two sides of the contest thus formed; it was organized religion against secular society.[11] Those against abortions were pro-life, and those for abortions were pro-choice.

In 1973, the matter was settled by the Supreme Court of the United States. It faced the difficult problem of balancing two conflicting values; that is, protection of the unborn, which disfavors abortion, and preserving the right of privacy for the woman, which favors abortion. There is no absolute answer to this question; it is an irreconcilable dilemma. The question does, however, bring up the matter of viability which is the gestational age after which the fetus has a reasonable chance of surviving outside the womb. That age had been the legal border between the earlier period during which abortion had been acceptable, and the later period during which the procedure had been illegal.

It happens that viability is a span of time rather than a specific time. Viability begins at about the beginning of the third trimester. The earliest time is 23-24 weeks of gestation.[12] Before that the fetal lungs are not sufficiently mature to support respiration. However, at that gestational age the incidence of developmental defects is high. As gestational age advances, developmental defects decrease, so the optimal time for high survivability and low incidence of defects is not clear-cut. The Supreme Court had to make a judgment on this question.

On January 22, 1973, the decision was announced. Associate Judge Harry Blackman wrote the opinion which was approved 7 to 2 by the full Court. The ruling was that, in the case of Roe v. Wade, the state must allow abortions in the first trimester of pregnancy. In the second trimester, the state could regulate abortions only to ensure that the procedure be performed safely, and in the third trimester, when the fetus had become viable, the state would allow abortions only when a continued pregnancy would be life-threatening. Thus, Roe v. Wade opened up legal abortions to the millions of women who had previously subjected themselves to the black market procedure with its attendant health risks.

The Court's decision was based mainly on the constitutional right of privacy, a fundamental right, which allows the woman to decide for herself whether to have an abortion. It also represented a compromise between the woman's interest in reproductive choice by allowing early abortions, and the state's interest in protecting fetal life by disallowing abortions in the third trimester.

The ruling was immediately followed by a storm of controversy. It became a contest between organized religion on the one hand, and secular society on the other. Speaking for organized religion, Catholic leaders immediately denounced the Roe decision.[13] Religious groups portrayed it as government sponsored mass killing.[14]

In the year of the decision, the Catholic church spent four million dollars lobbying Congress against Roe v. Wade; and, in 1974, Cardinals Krol, Medeiros, Cody, and Manning testified in favor of a pro-life constitutional amendment before Senator Birch Bayh's Senate Judiciary Subcommittee on Constitutional

Amendments. Prior to that, no Catholic cardinal had ever testified before a congressional committee.[15]

Some of the arguments against abortion became emotional. For example, Randall Terry, founder of Operation Rescue, and a zealous anti-abortion activist, declared that married couples who confess to be followers of the Lord Jesus should leave the number of children they have in the hands of God.[16] Jerry Falwell also spoke for religion. He said that he believed that Satan had mobilized forces to destroy America by negating the Judeo-Christian ethic, secularizing society, and devaluating human life through legalizing abortion and infanticide. He felt that God needed voices raised to save the nation from moral decay.[17] Others pointed out that abortion violated the fetus' right to life.[18] Still others characterized abortion as a tool of Satan.[19] The Catholic church held abortion to be evil, and a form of murder.[20] And finally, the church spoke again, declaring that all humans are made in the image of God, and all humans have immortal souls, as if an abortion would be an offense to God.[21]

While these incisive criticisms were being lodged by the pro-life groups, the pro-choice rebuttals seemed somewhat weaker. They emphasized that legalizing abortion reduces the illegal abortions which affect especially the poor; they preserve the autonomy of the woman; and, they disallow the birth of unwanted children.

However, two considerations tend to strengthen the pro-choice position. The first deals with the question of whether or not there is a deity. Since there is no evidence to suppose that a deity exists, the assertions of the churches, Catholic or Protestant, are considerably weakened. In the absence of a deity, the clergy is deprived of authority in the matter. Without a deity, the issue is no longer one of religion. The so-called church scholars, various popes, and televangelists speak without evidence, and with no more authority or wisdom than the lay public. And Jerry

Falwell, wanting to please God by disallowing abortions, finds himself in the awkward position of not having a God to please. The abortion debate is not a religious problem.

The second consideration is that it's not a religious question, it's a moral problem. It's a question of what's best for society. Is society better off with abortions or without abortions? That is a problem for the public to confront because the clergy has no monopoly on moral questions.

How can this matter be decided? Considering the consequences helps. If abortions are prohibited, the woman with an unwanted pregnancy has three options. The first is to carry the pregnancy to term, often at the cost of social disgrace, and bring an unwanted child into society. That is an indelible blight on the woman, the child, and society.

The second is to relinquish the baby to strangers, enter a too hasty marriage, or struggle as a single parent with a child branded as illegitimate, although not publicly now. The third is to seek a black market abortion with its high frequency of health risks including hemorrhage, pelvic infection, perforation of the uterus, shock, and death. Although without abortions, fetuses are saved, but catastrophic burdens are heaped on the other parties.

If abortions are allowed, all of these burdens on the woman, the child, and society are avoided. However, the conceptus is sacrificed. Since about 90 per cent of abortions are performed in the first trimester (12 weeks), some of that sacrificed is hardly more than a cluster of undifferentiated embryonic cells.[22] Also, the ability to think is said not to develop until the 24th to 27th week of gestation.[23] Therefore, the life lost is often not yet a sentient being.

How many of these should be given up for an adult woman in her early years with most of her life still ahead of her? Which takes precedence, the fetus or the adult? Many would say the latter. So while there is no perfect solution to the abortion problem, the benefits to the woman, the child, and society are vastly greater with the allowance of abortions than with the prohibition of them.

♦ ♦ ♦ ♦ ♦

CHAPTER 10 REFERENCES

1. Judges, D.P. *Hard Choices, Lost Voices.* Ivan R. Dee, Chicago, 1993, p. 84.
2. Cavanagh, D. "Abortion." *Encyclopedia Americana.* 1: 44, 1998.
3. Ibid., p. 44.
4. Ibid., p. 44.
5. Ibid., p. 45.
6. Ibid., p. 43.
7. O'Brien, D.M. "Abortion." *The World Book Encyclopedia.* 1: 14, 1998.
8. Judges, D.P., p. 84.
9. O'Brien, D.M., p. 15.
10. Tribe, L.H. *Abortion: The Clash of Absolutes.* W.W. Norton & Company, New York, 1990, p. 51.
11. Judges, D.P., p. 12.
12. Ibid., p. 62.
13. Tribe, L.H., p. 139.
14. Ibid., p. 141.
15. Ibid., p. 145.
16. Judges, D.P., p. 13.
17. Falwell, J. *Strength for the Journey. An Autobiography.* Simon and Schuster, New York, 1987, p. 362.
18. Schur, E. M. "Abortion." *Encyclopedia Americana.* 1: 44, 1998.
19. Judges, D.P., p. 14.
20. Tribe, L.H., p. 143.
21. "Ethics. Abortion, Euthanasia, and the Value of Human Life." *The New Encyclopedia Britannica* (Macropedia). 18: 518, 1994.
22. Costa, M. *Abortion: A Reference Handbook.* ABC-CLIO, Santa Barbara, California, 1991, p. 91.
23. Judges, D.P., p. 60.

11

Homosexuality is a legitimate lifestyle.

Homosexuality, HIV, and AIDS

HOMOSEXUALITY IS AN ISSUE OVER which the secular and theological communities sharply differ. It is defined as a sexual orientation to a person of one's own sex. Male homosexuals are commonly known as gays, and women as lesbians. Homosexuals are found in all cultures throughout the world, large or small, ancient or modern, and advanced or primitive. All degrees, from exclusively homosexual to exclusively heterosexual, occur. Social attitudes toward this lifestyle vary from strict prohibition to casual acceptance to active encouragement. Homosexuals may be happy or neurotic, faithful or promiscuous, gentle or aggressive, and may exhibit any degree of bisexuality. While figures are not precise, it is estimated that in the United States, ten per cent of men and five per cent of women are homosexual.[1] Throughout the Christian era, the homosexual lifestyle has been scorned, and persons with this orientation have been rudely rejected and treated as pariahs.

The cause is unknown. In 1935, Freud wrote that it is nothing to be afraid of, it is no vice, and it cannot be classified as an illness.[2] In 1974, the Diagnostic and Statistical Manual of the American Psychiatric Association removed it from its list of illnesses.[3] Freud regarded it as an arrest of sexual development that cannot be cured. By 1998, the encyclopedia described the condition as one that amounted to only a "tendency to be sexually or romantically attracted to members of one's own sex."[4] Nevertheless, the clergy has condemned homosexuality, has treated it as an optional and immoral choice of the individual, and has caused untold suffering to people who are basically "just trying to find out who they are."[5]

While he was still in Poland, Cardinal Wojtyla condemned homosexuality as a perversion, and after he became Pope John Paul II, he proclaimed same-sex love as an intrinsic moral evil.[6] Also, he lectured Archbishop Raymond Hunthausen of Seattle, who ministered acceptingly to homosexuals, that homosexuality and premarital sex are "incompatible with God's plan for human love."[7] Pat Robertson, the American televangelist, also spoke of homosexuality as an abomination, a perversion.[8]

These criticisms were made before various studies indicated that homosexuality may be due to hormonal or genetic factors. Since this disclosure, such criticisms have been less frequent. Nevertheless, it suggests that so long as a practice is regarded as optional and is morally objectionable, the clergy will authoritatively declare it a sin, but as soon as the lifestyle is found to be unavoidable, the assured authority of the church evaporates. The clerics appear to be certain only about that which is inexplicable.

In contrast, secular voices remain unknowing about that for which there is no evidence, and otherwise speak with only the authority the evidence allows. Whatever the cause of homosexuality, the condition remains a life-long orientation.

In June of 1981, five sexually active young homosexual males became ill with a pneumonia that was due to the uncommon parasite, Pneumocystis carinii. That organism is found in patients with suppressed immune systems. Soon thereafter, 26 additional male homosexuals were found to have an unusual malignant tumor that is known as Kaposi's sarcoma. It also occurs in those with suppressed immune systems. These two sets of patients announced the beginning of one of humankind's worst epidemics. The illness is contagious, occurs in both homosexuals and heterosexuals, affects men and women, is characterized by a suppressed immune system, and is uniformly fatal. It is termed acquired immunodeficiency syndrome or AIDS.

The cause of AIDS was a virus that arose in Africa, was transported to Haiti, and then entered the United States. In the beginning it affected mainly male homosexuals. Once in the body, the virus multiplies in monocytes and macrophages which are unaffected, and act as a reservoir for the organism. The genetic material of HIV is RNA (ribonucleic acid) which is converted to DNA by an enzyme, reverse transcriptase. The DNA is then integrated into the nuclear material of the cell, and it multiplies with the cell every time it divides. It cannot be removed from the cell, and for this reason, the patient is infected for life.

Later, the virus destroys the T-lymphocytes in the blood causing those cells to drop in number from a normal range of 8000 to 1500 per cmm. (cubic millimeter) to less than 500 cells per cmm. With reduced T-lymphocytes, the immune system is crippled. The infective agent is labeled a human immunodeficiency virus or HIV. No other infective agent causes such a pronounced collapse of the immune system.[9]

The HIV enters the body through the contaminated needles of drug users, by transfusions of contaminated blood, or by passage of the newborn through an infected birth canal. The most common route, however, is a cut or abrasion on skin or a mucosal surface, usually oral, anal, or on the sexual organs. The abrasion heals and the patient regards himself/herself, as well. There is no way to identify the infection until antibodies appear in the blood one to six months later.[10] When antibodies are found, the patient is said to be HIV positive. He/she is not sick, however, and may remain clinically well for 8 to 15 years. During this "silent" time, in ignorance of the disease, the virus may be passed to others. The patient will continue to be infective for the rest of his/her life.

Because of this "silent" period, the disease may spread widely without the knowledge of the sexual participants. Between 1985 and 1988, cancer deaths in the United States fell two per cent, and deaths from heart disease were down eight per cent. During the same period, deaths from AIDS surged 175 per cent.[11] The same authors also reported that more Americans have died of AIDS than died in the Viet Nam and Korean wars combined.[12]

At the end of this so-called "silent" period, AIDS develops. The clinical manifestations are protracted fever, weight loss that may become pronounced, chronic diarrhea, mucosal ulcers, and widespread enlargement of lymph nodes. There are also fatigue, lethargy, and depression. Because the immune system is suppressed, opportunistic infections complete the syndrome with cytomegalovirus pneumonia, Pneumocystis carinii pneumonia, tuberculosis, or shingles. Tumors may also arise, especially Kaposi's sarcoma, and lymphomas. Death occurs in 18 months to two years after the clinical onset.

The pastoral duties of the clergy bring them in contact with AIDS patients who, for the most part, have acquired their infections through practices that are unacceptable to some religions. Those practices have been scorned by the Christian religion for the past 2,000 years. At the same time, AIDS patients may yearn to return to religion but fear its stern dictates against homosexuality. Also, some of the churches may oppose those measures that are aimed at controlling the AIDS epidemic, such as the distribution of condoms and explicit education about the disease, which may be regarded as pornographic. The clergy is thus caught between the sexual practices they oppose, and their traditional role of caring for the ill and providing shelter for those society has abandoned.

It appears to be an incompatibility that cannot be resolved. If the clergy accepts homosexual practices, they feel immorality will prevail; and, if those practices are condemned, a segment of society will be left without the ministry of a church. A choice has to be made between the two. It is much better to side with a legitimate segment of society than it is to condemn and cast out that segment.

Is homosexuality legitimate? Of course it is; it is an innocent orientation not even regarded as an illness by physicians. Therefore, the clergy, while it means well, has no right to deny and curtail the sexual practices of the homosexual community. Instead of being condemnatory, the clergy should minister to the homosexuals, not in terms of obedience to a presumed deity, but in terms of compassion and guidance for those caught between an irrevocable but legitimate lifestyle on the one hand, and a traditional but opposing moral conviction on the other. The clergy should also support those practices that help to control the AIDS epidemic. These include information about the disease, preventive measures, the use of condoms, and acceptance of a lifestyle it cannot avoid.

In choosing between the moral convictions of the churches, and the legitimate needs of the homosexuals, it is the former that fails to meet the public need. Rejecting homosexuality on the basis of a synthetic definition of morality is as preposterous as the notion that AIDS is God's retribution for being homosexual.

If there were ever a segment of society in need of solace and compassion and shelter and approval, it is the homosexuals. The churches should extend their care and compassion to them in the same degree that it ministers to those with other illnesses. It is the secular community that has had the maturity and wisdom and compassion to stand up in support of all legitimate groups in society, regardless of the degree to which their practices are disparate.

· · · · ·

CHAPTER 11 REFERENCES

1. Konner, M. "Homosexuality." *Encyclopedia Americana.* 14: 333, 1998.
2. Ibid., p. 334.
3. Ibid., p. 334.
4. Ibid., p. 333.
5. Ibid., p. 334.
6. Kwitny, J. *Man of the Century: The Life and Times of Pope John II.* Henry Holt and Company, New York, NY 10011, 1997, p. 570.
7. Ibid., p. 534.
8. Donovan, J.B. *Pat Robertson: The Authorized Biography.* MacMillan Publishing Co., New York, 1988, p. 195.
9. Schoub, B.D. *AIDS and HIV in Perspective.* Cambridge University Press, New York, 1994.
10. "HIV" *Encyclopedia Americana.* 1: 366, 1998.
11. Martelli, L.I., Pelz, F.D., Messino, W., and Petro, S. *When Someone You Know Has AIDS.* Crown Publishers, Inc., New York, 1993, p. 8.
12. Ibid., p. 7.

12

Prisons are hate factories.

Controlling Crime

A MAIN TEACHING OF THE CHRISTIAN CHURCH in contemporary matters is forgiveness. Yet in the treatment of crime, punishment is accepted, and the more serious the crime, the more severe the punishment. The punishments are called the consequences, but in reality are now verging on revenge.

There are those who will argue that without Christianity crime conditions will worsen. But can they? Crime is certainly an outstanding problem for American society. Over the past two decades it has increased in frequency and seriousness; it has flourished especially among juveniles; and, it has required the construction of new prisons at high expense. Nevertheless, prison facilities are still inadequate, and felons are being sent back to the streets before their sentences are completed.

The re-arrest rates for juveniles in Florida are reported to range from 55 per cent for minor offenses, to 71 per cent for more serious crimes.[1] In confronting this problem, the public attitude is to get tough on crime, and punishments are made more severe. An example of this is the recent sentencing of a 36 year old gang killer to life imprisonment.[2] It is not just the life sentence, but the condition that all of it would be spent in solitary confinement. That means 23 hours of each day in a 7 by 12 foot cell, food shoved through a slot in the door, and no visitors, save his lawyer and close relatives, of which he has none.

A Harvard psychiatrist commented that he can imagine a sober society living with capital punishment, but he can't imagine a civilized society living with the punishment of driving a prisoner insane. And a Hofstra Law School professor remarked that no matter how horrible the crime, there are humane limitations to punishment.[2]

Another example is the bill recently before Congress, "The Juvenile Crime Control Act of 1999," which proposes to treat juvenile offenders over 13 as adults.[3] The bill has not yet become law, but courts are already making case by case decisions to do this. However, juvenile crime and recidivism continue unabated. Something is seriously wrong.

The root of the problem lies in attitudes that translate into acts and then into consequences. The two types of attitude are positive and negative. The former expresses goodwill and includes friendship, trust, and love. The latter expresses ill will and includes anger, distrust, and dislike. The main point is that a positive or good act will generally elicit a positive or good response, whereas, a negative or bad act will generally elicit a negative or bad response. An act and the response to it are of the same kind.

This fundamental truth may be challenged. For example, the parent spanks the child. It is a negative act that causes discomfort and sometimes pain. As a result the child stops misbehaving. It may therefore be claimed that a negative act has caused a positive response. This, however, is a misinterpretation.

The child quickly sees that to continue to misbehave only increases the punishment to which he/she is subjected. After all, he/she is small, weak, and unarmed; whereas, the adult administering the punishment is big, strong, and armed with belt or paddle. Therefore, he/she desists, but silently resents the treatment, and vows to retaliate in some way when he/she can. Thus, the spanking has not persuaded her/him to behave; it has persuaded her/him to misbehave when he/she can get away with it and not be punished.

This is illustrated by the report of a juvenile who was punished for a minor offense. Asked what he had learned from the experience, he replied, "I guess if I do something again, I'll try not to get caught."[4] It's also indicated by the American Medical Association, which points out that spanking can lead to antisocial and even violent behavior in later years.[5]

Parents, on the other hand, presume success since the child has stopped misbehaving. This convinces them of the usefulness of punishment. They further presume that if the misbehavior is repeated, the punishment should be increased to cause more discomfort. The adults thus make two mistakes; one, that the child has learned a lesson; and, two, that if the misbehavior is repeated, the punishment should be more severe. Both are wrong; the child develops resentment rather than compliance, and this effect is compounded by increasing the severity of the punishment. Thus, spanking is not an example of a negative act producing a positive result. That is rationally not possible.

This lesson applies to larger matters. When the male felon is accused of a crime and is found guilty, he is put in prison. There he is strip-searched, changed into drab prison garb, and shoved into a small concrete cell with steel bunks, an open toilet, and unshaded lights. Often there is no ventilation, no window, virtually no privacy, and only steel bars to peer through. His guards may be surly, and his food is unpalatable. He may have a cell mate he neither knows nor likes.

In reporting on a new prison in Oklahoma, reporter Kuntz describes windowless rooms, cramped quarters, and inadequate ventilation for inmates who are caged therein for 23 hours per day on weekdays, and 24 hours per day on weekends.[6] If the prisoner misbehaves, he will be manhandled with handcuffs, leg irons, truncheons, straight jackets, and solitary confinement. He may work on gangs with other inmates shackled together like so many animals. Many feel this treatment is degrading, inhumane, and unworthy of a civilized society.

A further example of severe treatment is capital punishment. This frightful act of legal murder is the most extreme expression of ill will. It is also the most extreme act of vengeance. It has never been proven as a factor in deterring those who might otherwise commit a serious crime. Of this, two points may be made. The first is that capital punishment does not serve any purpose that cannot be served equally well by the more civilized penalty of life imprisonment. The second is that there is, "...no useful evidence on the deterrent effect of capital punishment."[7]

It cannot be denied that a man subjected to capital punishment cannot repeat his crime. Nor can it be denied that the rate of crime is low in countries where punishments are severe, such as cutting off a man's hand for thieving. These 'successes,' however, come at a price. They require the abandonment of mercy, a disregard for compassion, and a willingness to replace harm with harm. It prostitutes the character of a country. The soul of a nation should not be disfigured by its treatment of crime. A punishment that serves only vengeance is not worthy of a civilized culture.

The consequence of this barbarity is that the prisoner becomes bitter toward society, he thinks of vengeance instead of rehabilitation, and he becomes a "hardened criminal." He becomes a career criminal, and prison becomes a school for crime. Recidivism rises. More prisons have to be built. Expense rises. That the nation might become prison poor, is a serious problem being written about now. The whole system is out of control. It is another example of presuming that a negative act (punishment) can cause a positive result (rehabilitation). There has to be more to prison experience than harsh punishment for turn around behavior on the part of the prisoner.

This dilemma of the prisoner was expressed by an inmate who wrote to his wife about such matters. He wrote, "For my teaching assignment I earn $1.30 a month. Many of the men here receive no funds from home and they cannot even spend their meager earnings until they have accumulated fifteen dollars to their account. If I seem bitter I just cannot hide it. When a man is turned out to society (over 99 per cent return) many of them have only $20.00 with which to start again. The hostility of society on the outside only makes them resentful. I have talked with many of them who have returned to the institution with a 'What's the use? They don't want me outside.' To them it is hell here and hell on the outside."[8] And society has a crime cost that is exceeded only by the cost of national defense.

Why isn't our research on human motivation and human behavior being used to solve this problem? Why do we let the failures of society become the keepers of our prisoners? Is it not clear that punishment and physical and psychological sadism against offenders only increase the tensions and frustrations of the prisoner, leaving no time for positive thought?

While justice muddles along with this mistaken idea of ill will stimulating goodwill, resolution of the problem comes into view. It is to abandon the act of ill will, which is punishment. This at first appears radical, but it is necessary to consider because the dimensions of the problem are so great. In place of these degrading, and, it might be said, self-defeating acts of inhumanity, the prisoner is incarcerated not for punishment, but for the protection of the public. The prisoner accepts this, and the public demands it.

Since punishment is out, reasonable comforts should be in. These include palatable meals, exercise equipment, card games, a desk with writing equipment, access to a library, a covered latrine, shaded lights, air conditioning, a window with a view, vocational guidance, and even college level courses with reduced sentences for earned degrees for those who will leave. Soft music during certain hours of the day, and a weekly movie are not out of the question. Computer instruction would be useful, as it has been elsewhere.[9] Psychological counseling should be available. Guards' behavior should be professional.

Everything should be done to restore dignity and self-worth. The prisoner learns that the state is compassionate. The state becomes a caring agency. This change, pronounced as it is, turns on the fundamental conviction that only a positive act will generate a positive result. Society, as well as the inmate, thus benefit from the prison experience.

In addition to this philosophy, the inmate is given a rewarding opportunity. He is advised that as soon as he can convince a parole board that he is rehabilitated, he may return to society. He returns on parole, of course, but he has achieved a large measure of freedom which is important to him. It is this offer that gives him the incentive to improve.

While the prisoner is no longer punished, his life is not altogether easy. He still spends several hours each day locked in a small cell, he is still denied conjugal visits, and he is still regimented unendingly. It is a confining existence in which he is denied his freedom.

The abandonment of punishment raises certain questions. Foremost among these is whether the public is safe. The public is protected to the degree that rehabilitation is valid. Of course, some wrong-doer may feign rehabilitation and then repeat a crime. However, this is unlikely for two reasons. The first is that the wrongdoer knows that a second incarceration will be prolonged because the public has to be protected. The second is that he has been treated so well in prison that his antagonism toward the state has dissolved. In the place of his antisocial inclination, he has developed a sense of self-worth so that his objective is to function within society as a law-abiding citizen rather than outside it as a criminal. The new program thus protects the public from both more crime and more recidivism.

The public is also protected by the knowledge that some criminals cannot avoid repeating their crimes. These are the hardened criminals, the pedophiles, and the serial killers. Such deviates will have to be incarcerated unendingly because they cannot be cured of their habits and the public has to be protected. This is not inhumane, however, because the in-house conditions are so decent. Besides, permanent incarceration under these conditions is better than returning a deviate to society and then advertising to the public his whereabouts and his crimes.

There is also the question of expense. It turns out that the cost of the accommodations outlined above are slight compared with those of punishment. Huge expense is incurred when prison riots cause fire, the wholesale destruction of property, and the loss of lives of both prisoners and guards. It is reported that in Venezuela, 29 inmates died in a prison riot in 1998. Some were beheaded.[10] The cost of rehabilitation is comparatively slight; it is punishment that is expensive.

Another question is how mandatory sentences are reconciled with early parole. In the new program, the period of incarceration is no longer fixed and mandatory. Instead, it is flexible, and is determined more by the progress of the rehabilitation than by the seriousness of the crime. It is axiomatic that rehabilitation presumes a crime will not be repeated. Therefore, no gain is derived from further incarceration. After all, incarceration is not for punishment; it is for the protection of the public.

The inmate may choose to stay in jail at public expense because the conditions are so comfortable. In this case the public will have to stand the expense because it deserves the protection that jail-time provides. Such a choice is unlikely, however.

The prisoner has only two options; he can remain in jail without freedom, or he can rehabilitate himself and achieve freedom. Seldom will he choose the former.

The final question is whether the public will accept the absence of punishment. Society equates punishment with justice in an 'eye for an eye' tradition. The idea is to make the punishment fit the crime. However, this tradition expresses vengeance, and vengeance is an unworthy goal. It helps neither the offender nor the victim. The public loss is, therefore, negligible. Reports on those relatives who finally witness the execution of the person responsible for their loved one's death are consistent in relating that the witnesses do not feel closure or relief and need to heal in other ways.

For the first time the prisoner is given not punishment, but an incentive to improve. For the first time the prison experience is self-correcting rather than socially antagonizing. That is extremely important because over 90 per cent of prisoners sooner or later return to society. Without such a program, society is becoming overwhelmed by an escalating prison population and a rising rate of recidivism. Prisoners are warehoused and released, often in worse mental condition than when they entered. It is a major improvement to transform the treatment of crime from a negative experience in which bitterness thrives and crime is repeated, to a positive experience in which the criminal actually learns to live crime-free.

It is thus evident that in some measure crime can be controlled. The bold stroke is to eliminate punishment. This allows reward for good behavior to replace punishment for bad behavior. The former is superior because it allows an act of goodwill (decent incarceration) to evoke a response of goodwill (rehabilitation). In fact, it pressures the prisoner in the right direction; if he/she fails to rehabilitate, he/she is penalized by further incarceration. If he/she does rehabilitate, he/she is rewarded with parole.

Thus, the new system is more humane than punitive; it decreases crime and repeat-crime; it reduces the need for more prisons, lessens the cost of operation, rehabilitates prisoners, and brings men back into the civil order. All of this is accomplished without sacrificing the protection of the public. With so much to gain, and so little to lose, the program ought to be considered and tried.

♦ ♦ ♦ ♦ ♦

CHAPTER 12 REFERENCES

1. Ruane, D. "Juvenile Offenders Pack Centers." *News-Press.* Ft. Myers, FL, Sept. 1, 1997.
2. *New York Times*, Oct. 26, 1997, p. 24.
3. White, D. Debate, "Decisions Should Be Kept at Home." *News-Press.* Ft. Myers, FL, Sept. 2, 1997.
4. *New York Times Magazine*, Oct. 26, 1997, p. 24.
5. Ryan, R. "AMA Study: Spare the Rod, Save the Child." *News-Press.* Ft. Myers, FL, Aug. 15, 1997.
6. Kuntz, T. "A Grim Glimpse of Oklahoma's Thoroughly Modern Death Row." *New York Times*, Jan. 15, 1995.
7. Bedau, H. M., Editor. *The Death Penalty in America.* Third Edition. Oxford University Press, New York, 1982.
8. Personal letter to Chandler Smith, the author.
9. Associated Press. "Education Offers Prisoners Self-esteem." *News-Press."* Ft. Myers, FL, Oct. 19, 1997.
10. Associated Press. "Venezuela Inmates Tell of Hellish Prison Riot." *The Sunday Oregonian.* Portland, OR, Sept. 28, 1997.

13

*As long as nations bear
arms, war is inevitable.*

The Impossibility of Peace

ANY DISCUSSION ON PEACE should begin by considering conscience because it's important to know what it is and what causes it. When the infant is born, it is hugged and kissed and caressed by its caretakers, most often the parents, who lavish love and care and sweetness on the baby. This continues through the early years during which the child learns love, trust, honesty, friendliness, and goodwill, as well as mistrust, dishonesty, dislike, anger, and sometimes hate. Thus, in these formative years, the youngster learns about right and wrong, which we'll call morality.

In this process he or she develops conscience. An essential point is that conscience is not a spark of divinity that lights the soul; it has nothing to do with religion. It is engendered by the early, human bonding, and it is necessary for a peaceful life in a communal setting. It has always been needed; society cannot survive without love and goodwill and the other virtues of conscience.

This said, it becomes apparent that only three different responses can be made to aggression, especially aggression in the form of violence, which is action that is void of love, goodwill, and the virtues of conscience. The ways are: retaliation, which forms one pole of the spectrum; surrender, which forms the other pole, and, a midpoint that neither retaliates nor surrenders. There are no other different ways. These responses form a spectrum as shown in Figure G.

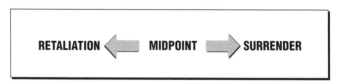

Fig. G. The three different responses to violence. There are no others.

The popular understanding is that if one side didn't fight, it had to surrender. The spectrum disallows that thought. There are three different ways and only three. In fact, the midpoint means nonviolence, a hard word to use because in some circles it tends to send listeners scurrying for the exits. However, nonviolence does not say nonsurrender, so it does not imply a spectrum. The word I've used escapes the stigma of nonviolence, suggests a spectrum, and implies non-surrender, too, rendering it preferable.

There are no other ways of contending with violence. A person who retaliates against an aggressor may use a knife to stab, a bomb to destroy, a gun to shoot, or a poison to kill. While these are different, they are all examples of retaliation. In the same way, the individual who surrenders may pay money to the attacker, may give up land, may abandon jewelry or other valuables, or may promise never to speak against the offender. Each of these differs from the others, but all are examples of surrender. Taken in this categorical way, only the three different responses cited are possible.

When a person retaliates, the extreme of that response is to kill the attacker. Once that's done, retaliation has no further purchase. After the attacker is killed, there's no point in burning his house down. Dispatch of the attacker is the extreme of retaliation. Once that's done, there is nothing more to do.

On the other end of the spectrum is surrender. It also has a limit. Surrender comes in all degrees, but when it is total and abject, there is nothing beyond that. After all is given up, there is nothing more to give. That is the absolute limit. This leaves us with a spectrum of responses to violence that is bounded on both ends. That is, retaliation has an absolute limit, and surrender has an absolute limit. Both have endpoints that cannot be exceeded. This is important because it means that we have limitations on what we can do in response to violence. There are no other different ways. Moreover, the spectrum is as solid as a mountain of granite. It can't be changed, ever. It's independent of time. It's a prison; the whole human family is imprisoned within the spectrum.

In thinking about this it is helpful to realize that the physical sciences have only a few absolute constants. The best example is the speed of light which is absolutely invariant at 186,000 miles per second. Since the world is 25,000 miles around, the speed of light is about seven times around the world in one second. But the rate isn't so important as the fact that it is absolutely constant.

The social sciences are different. They have no units that can be weighed, measured, or expressed in numbers. For this reason they are known as the soft sciences. However, the spectrum of responses to violence, while not a physical measurement, is nevertheless an absolute constant. It is a limitation that cannot change.

Historically, the ultimate response to violence has been violence (retaliation), with wars happening somewhere on earth at all times. It is always a major problem facing mankind. War is not what it used to be due to the scientific progress in manufacturing weapons. In the past, mankind has faced war and has always survived, even though society has been convulsed by it. For over 60 years we have had nuclear weapons, and they are owned by several nations. As the years go by, others will acquire them. Since nuclear war might destroy all of civilization, it is relevant to know the limits of what can be done. Only with this knowledge can the best plan of action be found. That's why the spectrum is important.

In considering the spectrum, there is neither retaliation nor surrender at the midpoint. What it does is to stand steady, express disapproval of wrongdoing, and neither take up weapons nor run away. It means the avoidance of killing, which is retaliation, and the avoidance of running away, which is surrender.

Here it is important to emphasize that the two ends of the spectrum are equally bad. Surrender abandons principle, offers no resistance to wrongdoing, relinquishes honor, and is cowardly. It is unthinkable. It is not in the American arsenal of tactics in the case of war. Our concentration is with retaliation at the other end of the spectrum. That tactic is based on the premise that life must be preserved at any cost. Once this premise is accepted, any means are justified in order to preserve life. This includes killing. So with this premise, we go to war with a clear conscience, and even ask God to bless our efforts. The rectitude of this response is found in long held tradition, and plain old common sense. In this way we justify war and prepare to convert the world into a global crematorium.

It's virtually certain that the traditionalists contemplating this will vehemently disagree. They will say that we've had wars all through history; we are almost always victorious in these matters; and, we now invest between two and three hundred billion dollars each year to assure ourselves that should war come, we will be victorious again. So to them, the traditional program appears sound.

There are two things wrong with the traditional program. The first is exemplified by General McArthur's statement that in war there is no substitute for victory. Therefore, whatever is needed to win will be used. In a few years most nations will have nuclear weapons. No nation at war is likely to accept defeat without using its maximum weapons. In this way, nuclear war becomes inevitable. Thus, in the silently approaching future, our program will fail, not only for us but for perhaps all of humanity as well. Is this the legacy we want to hand down? Is this the best that we, in our careful judgment, can recommend for mankind? Can we go forward with a program we know will fail? Perhaps we should think again.

The second thing wrong with the program is that it makes savages of us all. We cannot be savages. We must have a place in civilized society for love, compassion, tenderness, and goodwill. Society breaks down without these values. It is unacceptable to give them up.

But, the traditionalists again will come forward. They will say that if we give up retaliation, we are left with only surrender or the middle of the spectrum. Surrender is not acceptable; and, the middle means that without a fight, we will give up our lives.

Now, the tyranny of the spectrum becomes evident. None of the choices is safe. What do we do? Only we can decide. If we want to give up our honor, we surrender. That seems unthinkable. If we want to kill others in order to stay alive, then we take up our nuclear weapons. It is a tactic that can only fail. Failure lies at each end of the spectrum, and we cannot escape the spectrum. But if we take honor to be more important than life, then we stand in the middle, reject weapons altogether, object to evil peacefully, and take the consequences. Of course, it may be asked why we should take honor to be more important than life. After all, without life no one can do anything.

A long time ago a philosopher named Socrates made a

memorable comment. He said that the highest good is not life itself - mere survival, but a moral life. What he meant was that life alone allows for bad behavior. While Hitler lived, for example, atrocities were committed. We cannot accept that. It is only life lived honorably that is the highest good. That brings us back to the spectrum. Both ends are lacking in honor. It is only the center that is honorable.

It is hard for most to understand that peaceful objection to evil will eventually prevail, but the reason is that there lies in the human heart compassion and love. It was placed there by the nurturing caretakers as they cared for and loved their infants, not by a spark of religiosity. It is the habit and practice and experience of love that forms the model, so that in adult life harm and evil arouse revulsion and repugnance. The innocent cannot stand by and allow evil to run its course. Objection to evil will be raised even at the cost of physical harm Even at the cost of life!

What may come to mind is that Hitler was evil incarnate, and many may doubt that 'peaceful objection' would have deterred him. That's a perfectly natural thought. We are so bent on war, the production of ever greater armaments, the fight back mentality, and the glorification of our military, that it is almost impossible to conceive of, let alone accept, any response to violence other than retaliation.

Here the spectrum exerts its effect. If we see the wrong and the failure of retaliation, and if we see that it is as bad on its end of the spectrum as surrender is on its end, then we are forced to the only other possibility, which is the middle of the spectrum. The middle is the only tactic that allows us to escape the moral stain of killing others in order to stay alive, or the unthinkable rejection of honor that is surrender.

There are no other choices. Will we give up our lives in order to prevent murder and preserve honor, or will we take up weapons to kill others in the vain hope of preserving our own lives no matter what the cost to others? Seen in this light, the middle of the spectrum has advantages the military appears not to have foreseen.

It is difficult to believe that Hitler would have yielded. However, he would have been forced to because a successful program has to benefit the defender, and at the same time deprive the aggressor of something. For the defender, the midpoint rejects evil, preserves honor, and prevents war. Those are our objectives in responding at all. For the aggressor, it requires killing those who are unarmed, innocent, and non-threatening. That is lacking in courage and bravery. It is cowardly. No one can be proud of such behavior. Troops cannot have pride in their leader. They are sickened by his orders.

The middle tactic deprives the aggressor of an enemy. A leader can marshal his troops against an enemy that represents threat and danger, but he cannot marshal them against those who are innocent, unarmed, and non-threatening. Without an enemy, the leader loses the allegiance of his troops. The middle tactic isolates the leader from those he needs to obey his orders. There is nothing he can do; he cannot force the opponent to fight and thus become an enemy. The aggressor is deprived of leadership.

Hitler did kill millions of unarmed Jews. But, Hitler also convinced his people that the Jews were their enemies. Even before the Holocaust, Hitler expressed hate for the Jews, and even brought in God to help persuade his followers that the Jews were evil. In Mein Kampf he stated, "...I believe that I am acting in accordance with the will of the Almighty Creator: by defending myself against the Jew, I am fighting for the work of the Lord."[1] And the Jews did not go willingly to the gas chambers. They were scattered geographically, outnumbered, and victims of a secretive, evil behavior that seemed unimaginable in a civilized world. Their's was not a mid-spectrum behavior.

Wars have been going on since man began, and killing has been acceptable for self-defense. It's traditional and widely accepted. But think what it means. If we approve of retaliation for self-defense, then we are approving of violence; and, when masses of people approve of violence, it's the equivalent of approving of war. If the weapons are crude, as they have been in the past, the violence is limited; but, if the weapons are nuclear, as they are now, the violence is unlimited.

Civilization itself is at risk. When we say that we will kill, if necessary, to protect our own lives, what we are saying is that regardless of what happens to others, we will even sacrifice them to keep ourselves alive. That's why retaliation is about the most selfish and the most self-centered point of view possible. It's the equivalent of saying, "I'm willing to sacrifice civilization in order to protect myself."

It's nearly impossible to accept the midpoint as the best tactic, especially after these centuries of depending on retaliation; but, it is the best when the critical objective is to prevent war. Eventually, it would also mean dissemination of wealth in a more equitable way among individuals and nations, protection of the environment, control of the population, and reduction of our dependence on the military. The danger has been recognized. William Cohen, Secretary of Defense, in speaking about nuclear arms reduction, has said that our goal must be total elimination of those weapons.[2]

What's more likely to happen is that these ideas will be widely overlooked. Putting them in print is to draw heavy scorn. The military will continue to depend on fear by warning of imagined military encounters; and, the government will continue to fund ever more powerful weapons. Moreover, inequality among nations will continue. In short, nothing will change. We shall regard ourselves as the most powerful nation on earth at a time when excessive military force is accumulating all around us.

That is the consequence of not considering another tactic, such as the middle of the spectrum.

The preparation for war is sooner or later going to blow us up; the risk will increase until it all comes to an end. Peace cannot be achieved, even though it's possible, because the spectrum won't be recognized or followed. For some reason, individuals do not have the courage or the foresight to realize that in the event of using nuclear weapons, we must either give up our lives for the preservation of the human species, or we will all go down together.

An example can be made by taking the worst possible case. Suppose another Hitler were to come to power somewhere in Europe. He would be armed with nuclear weapons. After unacceptable military advances, war would become inevitable. The United States would have its own nuclear arsenal. Other nations, similarly armed, would line up with both of the major adversaries. Now what would the choices be? All out nuclear war would mean the end of civilization. We have to take that as a fact. Would we go to war and destroy ourselves and all of civilization, or would we lay down our weapons, object to evil, and take the consequences?

It is evident that this would mean a Hitler would rule the world. And, the former course, war, would mean that death would come to everyone. Some would as soon let civilization succumb as they would let Hitler dominate the world.

For discussion, say we were to lay down our weapons and take the consequences. It would be the only honorable course given the destruction of a nuclear war. Laying down weapons is not to be confused with surrender. It is not joining the enemy. It is saying that the enemy is absolutely wrong and we will have none of it, but will not cause irreparable harm, either. The enemy would then dispatch us and all like us. They would rule the world. What would that mean? It would mean that civilization would survive, that their administration would prevail - but, that sooner or later goodness would return because goodness is irrepressible. It can't be suppressed forever because it is part of the human condition.

A lifetime isn't very long. Things change. Goodness emerges. Goodwill returns. Civilization has something to build on. But if civilization is wiped out, nothing is left. It might take many millions of years for civilization to recover. So we have these choices: to abandon weapons, reject evil, preserve civilization, and give up our lives, if necessary, or to go to war, lose our lives, kill others, disown honor, and obliterate civilization. It would seem that most thoughtful and mature adults would make the former choice. It's honorable, and there's comfort in that. Besides, the killing of others and the wipe-out of civilization are hard to accept.

Of the three spectrum choices, we should take the one that is honorable, that does not require killing, that does not require surrender, that protects others, prevents war, and preserves society. Any person should be willing to give up life, if necessary, to accomplish this much. It is the price we have to pay to keep the human family alive.

❖ ❖ ❖ ❖ ❖

CHAPTER 13 REFERENCES

1. Hitler, A. *Mein Kampf.* Houghton Mifflin Company, Boston, MA, 1971, p. 65.

2. Carroll, J. "War Inside the Pentagon." *The New Yorker.* Aug. 18, 1997, p. 5.

14

*Retaliation is the reaction of fear;
nonviolence is the reaction of courage.*

Spectral Examples

IF THE RETALIATION - NONVIOLENCE - SURRENDER MODEL is sound, there ought to be some examples that verify it. In thinking about this, some come to mind.

Retaliation
   The premier example of retaliation is war. It's a beastly business. Men's skulls are crushed by rifle butts; their bodies are run through with bayonets; their throats are slashed with knives; their necks are throttled with wires; their guts are perforated with bullets; and, their parts are dismembered with bombs. They are shot out of the air and sea; and, they are gassed, tortured, and burned and buried alive. In future they may also starve, much as the million Russian children after they 'won' World War II. They may also freeze, and suffer the lingering death of radiation sickness, to say nothing of suicide, panic, terror, insanity, and death from biological agents.
   Both sides commit the same atrocities, and to perform such acts takes training. Moral customs have to be abandoned. A Marine chant at the Paris Island Training Center in 1982 included the following: "Number on deck, sir, forty five ... highly motivated, truly dedicated, rompin,' stompin,' blood thirsty, kill-

crazy United States Marine Corps recruits."[1] This is the condoning of unrestricted violence.

All of this depravity is practiced more or less evenly on both sides. After all, war is a kill or be killed situation. For the defeated, the psychological loss is great, in addition to everything else. The victorious, however, also suffer a loss. Their belief in the military and in retaliation becomes entrenched; and as soon as the bodies are cleared from the field, they begin the stockpiling of weapons so that in case of another war, they will succeed again.

Meanwhile, the defeated lick their wounds and think revenge. Both sides thus march resolutely into the jaws of hell. It is hard to make a favorable case for retaliation. That end of the spectrum is ignoble and deplorable, to say nothing of the fact that modern weapons destroy the opponents and the innocent onlookers, too.

Of course, retaliation may be employed with good intent. This does not change the negative aspect of the tactic, however. Consider the case of the Mexican bandit, Pancho Villa. He was born in Durango, Mexico in 1877.[2] He lived with his family in a hut on the edge of one of Durango's vast haciendas which was governed by rich landowners. The landowners were arrogant, powerful, and ruthless. They were the absolute rulers of the peasants who tilled their fields. When he was 12, Pancho's father died, and the young lad took over the responsibility for his family. While he could neither read nor write, and was dirt poor, he knew every cranny of the adjacent land including the ravines and caves in the nearby mountains.

When he was 16, a member of the ruling family attempted to defile his sister. His quick temper boiled over. Pancho raced home, grabbed his pistol, returned and shot the offender. He became an outlaw immediately and had to make for the hills he knew so well. He became a bandit and a revolutionary. His objective was to unseat the hated landowners and return the land to the peasants. In order to do this, and raise the peasants out of poverty, he looted trains, robbed banks, and raided mines.

Men joined him to overthrow the vicious landowners, and soon he was at the head of a revolutionary army. He challenged the leading politicians, winning some confrontations and losing some. In the beginning, thinking his cause was just, Woodrow Wilson supported him, but later, because of reports of brutality, gave up this association, and instead took up with Pancho's powerful opponent.

In 1926, feeling betrayed, Pancho raided the town of Columbus in New Mexico, burning the place to the ground and killing 18. President Wilson then dispatched an American force to New Mexico to capture the bandit. The commander of the force was Gen. John J. Pershing who crossed the border into Mexico to pursue him. But Pancho was too quick, and knew the country too well. After more than a year of searching, Gen. Pershing returned to the United States empty handed.

The people of Mexico resented Pershing's expedition, and raised Pancho Villa to the status of a folk hero. He made peace with the officials of the government, and was offered a handsome ranch if he would quit the political scene. He accepted, and appeared settled in a comfortable life. However, he had been a killer, and he had made enemies. The hatred was not forgotten, and in 1933, his enemies assassinated Pancho Villa. He was only 46.

The motivation for his revolutionary ways grew out of the inequality of arrogant wealth set against the squalor of grinding poverty; and, while the purpose of his revolution seemed just, a good intention does not escape the consequences of violence at the retaliatory end of the spectrum.

Surrender

On the other end of the spectrum, we come to surrender. It is equally as bad as retaliation, but it is not often resorted to because it is lacking in bravery and courage. All of the examples of surrender, so far as is known, are utter and complete failures. Some might say that to surrender in order to stay alive and fight another day is a victory, but the case is weak. In fact, it cannot succeed because success requires some objection to evil. In one case, however, surrender was glorified as an example of heroism and courage. The case is the Jewish event known as Masada.

Herod the Great was king of the Jews. His headquarters were in Jerusalem, and he was a cruel man. In order to find sanctuary from his unruly subjects, he built a mighty fortress on top of a high plateau that was located on the southwest corner of the Dead Sea. The plateau was flat on top, measured 2,000 by 950 feet, and was 1,300 feet above sea level with precipitous sides.

On this plateau Herod built cisterns for the storage of water, granaries for the storage of food, elaborate living quarters, a synagogue, bath houses, command posts, and administrative offices. He also built a double wall around the perimeter of the top for defense. It was an impregnable fortress and it was known as Masada.

Completed in about 30 B.C., it was the site of one of the most tragic events in Jewish history.[3] After its construction, the Romans conquered the area and occupied Jerusalem. They also attacked and overtook the Masada fortress. In 66 A.D. the Jews revolted against their oppressors, and during the revolt a small band of Jewish zealots attacked and conquered the Masada plateau. The company of zealots consisted of 900 men, women, and children. Stored food was sufficient for their needs, and a cache of arms was adequate for their defense. However, in 70 A.D. the revolt came to an end and the Romans re-occupied Jerusalem.

The Roman soldiers then decided to put an end to Masada, which became the last outpost of Jewish resistance. It was an enormous undertaking. The Roman company, numbering some 10,000, had to construct ramparts, defend them, and use battering rams, siege engines, rock bombardments, and flaming torches to overcome the 900 defenders, who operated from behind the double walls around the perimeter of the plateau. The defenders resisted mightily, and the siege lasted for five months. However, it finally became evident that the resistance could no longer hold out against the attack. The Romans knew, of course, that the defenders could not escape, so they settled down for the night and prepared to attack at dawn.

Inside the fortress the Jews were well aware of their dilemma. So they held a meeting at which their leader, Eliezer Ben-Yair made a long and impassioned speech. He pointed out that they did not want to be murdered by the Romans, and if not killed, they did not want to live as slaves. So he persuaded them to kill themselves, and what resulted was one of the largest mass suicides in history. The men selected ten of their number who were to be the executioners. The women and children lay down side by side in neat rows and bared their throats. When the executions were completed, the ten men selected one of them to execute the other nine and then run himself through with his own sword. The plan was carried out and completed.

The next morning the Romans, who were prepared to fight their way onto and over the plateau, were confronted by an eerie silence. The bodies were laid out in neat rows; there was no one to kill. Two women and five children hid in caves and survived. From them the story was learned. The attackers were impressed with the great courage of the defenders, and their fearless and utter contempt for death. So ended the Jewish resistance to Rome.

A cable car is now built to carry tourists and others to the top of the Masada plateau. It is second only to the Western (wailing) wall in Jerusalem as a tourist attraction. For Jewish youth, Masada is a symbol of courage, and each year the Jewish Armored Corps goes to the plateau to swear their allegiance to the armed forces by declaring that Masada shall not fall again.

Was this an example of heroism? It was certainly courageous, but perhaps not heroic. Surrender, which in this case was evidenced by quitting the field through suicide, cannot succeed because success requires resistance to evil. Suicide presents no resistance. They were courageous, but that alone was not enough. Success is defined by rejecting retaliation and surrender, and resisting the opponent, too. Otherwise, evil succeeds, except for retaliation, which is morally unacceptable and self-defeating as well.

Nonviolence

The last of the spectral choices is nonviolence. It is in the middle of the spectrum, and is the most difficult of the examples to find. The great proponents of nonviolence were, of course, Jesus, Gandhi, and M.L. King, Jr. All were killed, and it might thus appear that the tactic is of no value. That interpretation would be incorrect. Nonviolence can never lose because it prefers to give up life, if necessary, rather than resort to retaliation which endangers others, or turn to surrender, which fails to resist evil. It is only nonviolence that fulfills the definition of success; resisting evil while abstaining from both of the polar tactics of the spectrum. One might ask why it would be better to give up one's life rather than retaliate against the enemy. The answer is because retaliation requires killing, which is morally wrong, endangers others, and is self-defeating.

The counter argument is that it's no more wrong, morally, for you to kill them than it is for them to kill you. So that doesn't speak well against retaliation. But, there is another matter, with retaliation both sides become vicious savages. It isn't just that the weapons of today are overwhelming so that the opponents and the innocent bystanders are all killed; it's also the fact that culture, sophistication, and humaneness are all thrown out the window, leaving unscrupulous killing. Morality has to be preserved.

Animals are savages; they don't know about morality. But we humans, to be civilized, must cherish morality. Otherwise, all is lost.

The case is sound, but there is the question of whether anyone has the intestinal fortitude to accept death in order to preserve morality. The answer is that the first was Gandhi. He almost died by his own hand through fasting. He was prepared to give up his life in order to make those who followed him lay down their arms. He would have given up his life in order to put an end to violence. His work forced the British out of India. He did it without violence. He did it through the power of nonviolence. As a result, his extreme prominence in history is indelible.

The second was Martin Luther King, Jr. While he was killed, he was also prepared to give up his life for the sake of morality In fact, King said that a man who was not willing to die for something was not fit to live. He was awarded a Nobel Prize for his support of nonviolence, and for his defense of the black minority. It must be added, too, that the great defender of morality and the world's greatest proponent of nonviolence was Jesus Christ. When the Roman soldiers came for him, he did not run away, or commit suicide, or reach for arms in order to retaliate. Instead, he declared them wrong, forgave them for what they did, and without complaint accepted their cruelty. He died in agony, but he left an example the world has never forgotten, and can never overlook.

We rightly glorify him now, not because of a putative divinity, but because he resorted to the one tactic that rejected evil, turned away from retaliation, and abstained from surrender. That is the definition of success. That is the tactic that justifies his fame. We would do well to emulate him.

In a general way, people reject nonviolence. It's partly because we encourage retaliation so strongly. Programs run continuously on television glorifying the military, both the people and weapons. A popular motto of the military is "Be All You Can Be," as if it's an achievement to be able to kill several million human beings. It appears almost seditious to doubt the wisdom of war and the utility of weapons of mass destruction. But no matter how the case is made, when two nations both armed with nuclear weapons, face each other over an irreconcilable difference, war will result. Virtually any man facing death will prefer to use his nuclear weapons rather than give up his own life.

Nonviolence is also rejected because it's made to look cowardly. Actually anyone can pick up a weapon and kill one or many. That's done out of fear. It takes courage in the extreme to reject retaliation and surrender, the two poles of the spectrum, and prefer to give up one's life, if necessary, rather than plunge civilization into the abyss.

A position as extreme as nonviolence should have a sound explanation that all can understand. It was Gandhi who explained it when he wrote, "The strongest rebuke that can be levied against insolent tyranny is the willingness of the innocent to give up their lives in the defense of principle."[4] That may be one of the greatest sentences ever written. It will be the basis, sooner or later, for the preservation of all humanity. It thwarts the opponent altogether. The opponent is powerless to prevent one from objecting to evil, and from giving up life, if necessary, in support of his objection. The aggressor only soils its own reputation by further violence. Giving up one's life in objection to evil is the strongest possible rebuke that can be levied. Thus, it may be seen that retaliation is the reaction of fear, whereas, nonviolence is the reaction of courage.

The Spectrum

In this connection, we are back to the retaliation-nonviolence-surrender's three points; one on each side and one in the middle. It is also evident that the cross on which Jesus was crucified had three points, one on each side and one in the middle. If we think of retaliation as blood-soaked and cruel, and if we think of surrender as lacking in honor, then we might color retaliation red and surrender black to represent these aspects.

Accordingly, the cross might take on a variety of designs such as pins, lapel buttons, brooches, statues, or more formal constructions. The only key is that the lateral arms of the cross, or parts thereof, be colored red and black, and the central column be white. The red would represent the blood of retaliation, the black being for the dishonor of surrender, and the white for the central column of virtue. Here are some of the possibilities.

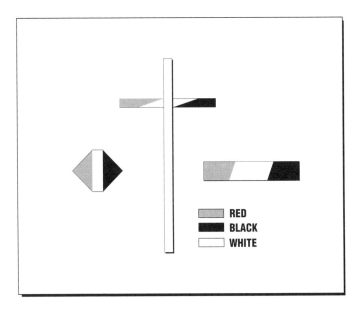

Fig. H. The Cross

CHAPTER 14 REFERENCES

1. Dyer, G. *War.* Crown Publishers, Inc., New York, 1985, p. 114.

2. Rouvenal, J. *Pancho Villa: A Biography.* Doubleday & Company, Inc. Garden City, New York, 1972.

3. Melrod, G. *Insight Guides: Israel.* Third Edition. Houghton Mifflin Co. Boston, MA, 1993.

4. Fischer, L. *The Life of Mahatma Gandhi.* Harper & Row, Publishers, New York, 1950.

15

Deterrence in the nuclear age fails if it is not used because it is morally obscene, and fails if it is used because it is self-defeating.

Deterrence

THE GENERAL CONSENSUS is that because war is futile, and nonviolence doesn't work, our attention should be focused on the prevention of war, which is deterrence. We in America are spending over 200 billion dollars every 365 days preparing for war. Those preparations are also for deterrence. With the threat of the use of nuclear weapons, maybe war can be put off forever.

It's a worthy topic because deterrence is a part of retaliation. Deterrence precedes retaliation, and retaliation comes into play only if deterrence fails. The problem is that deterrence doesn't seem to work. Deterrence, which means preventing through fear, defers war. It puts war off until a later time. We need something that will prevent war altogether. Deterrence is more or less reliable so long as all of the weapons are in the hands of the deterrer. When the arsenals are full on both sides, however, then the tactic is less reliable.

Deterrence is based on the adage, "If you seek peace, prepare for war." That, however, is a false message. It is possibly the most important and the most expensive false message of all time because war cannot be prevented by preparing for it. That is an oxymoron. George Kennan, former U.S. Ambassador to Russia, points out that arms races lead inexorably to war.[1] If there is one solid point against deterrence, it is that this tactic has not prevented war in the past. While prodigious efforts have been made to prevent war by preparing for war, wars nevertheless recur. It is this record of failure that speaks loudly against the expectation of success.

It was a man named Brodie, a graduate student at Yale, who initiated the idea of nuclear deterrence within a year of the Hiroshima bomb. That explosion killed 75,000 Japanese outright, and subsequently 130,000 succumbed to its effects. These awesome results caused Brodie to foresee that the atom bomb had changed the nature of warfare forever, and he realized that there could be no effective defense against such weapons. In 1946, he wrote, "Thus far the purpose of our military establishment has been to win wars. From now on, its chief purpose will be to avert them. It can have almost no other useful purpose."[2] Thus, the era of nuclear deterrence was born.

The subsequent history of deterrence is a checkered one. Brodie foresaw that only a small number of nuclear bombs would be sufficient to demolish a country, and therefore, the accumulation of a large number of such weapons would be superfluous. On that account, his theory was dubbed "Minimum Deterrence."

In 1954, John Foster Dulles, then the Secretary of State, discarded Brodie's idea, and announced a policy of "Massive Retaliation" in which the United States would depend primarily on a great capacity to retaliate.[3] Within one year, however, as Russian forces expanded, Dulles renounced his own doctrine.[4]

In 1958, the Navy approved a nuclear arsenal sufficient for deterrence but not adequate for the "...false goal of winning a nuclear war."[5] That proposal was titled, "Finite Deterrence." Not all approved. Paul Nitze, Vice Chairman of the U.S. Strategic

Bombing Survey for 1944-1946, recommended a policy of "Flexible Deterrence" in which a varied nuclear arsenal would allow strikes at small and large targets without necessarily setting off a global conflagration.[6]

President Eisenhower canceled this and left in office a top-secret "Single Integrated Operational Plan" (SIOP) in which the United States would release thousands of nuclear weapons on the Soviet Union and its allies.[7]

The next President, John Kennedy, abandoned this plan, and his Secretary of Defense, Robert McNamara, recommended targeting only military installations so that the fabric of society would be preserved. This was titled, "Assured Destruction." It was later changed to "Mutual Assured Destruction" or MAD. There were also other schemes, as the "Existential Deterrence" of McGeorge Bundy, Special Assistant to President Kennedy, and the "Minimum Assured Deterrent" of General Collins.[8,9] It appears that no one could find an enduringly satisfactory scheme for deterrence. In hindsight, that is not altogether surprising since it is hard to think of preventing something by preparing for it.

The initiators of all of these schemes were fully aware of nuclear parity with the other side. Thus, both parties knew that no matter which side struck first, the other side would always be able to inflict unacceptable damage by retaliation. It followed that "unacceptable damage" would be on the order of total destruction of the United States and total destruction of Europe. Deterrence is thus based on a threat that is self-destructive and, therefore, has scant credibility.

It was McNamara who stated that one cannot build a credible deterrent on an incredible action.[10] John Kenneth Galbraith, former U.S. Ambassador to India, also agreed with this view when he pointed out that military force no longer defended, it obliterated.[11] That a major war has not occurred over the past 50 years may be due in part to the terror of the weapons held by both sides; but of course, it is not possible to assign a cause-certain to a non-event.

The calm over the past 50 years is more likely due to the absence of an irreconcilable difference between two nations that were both armed with nuclear weapons. Nevertheless, other nations, and especially those of the Third World are acquiring such weapons. When the arsenals bulge on both sides, and the confrontation takes place, war will certainly occur. At that moment the failure of deterrence will become evident. Moreover, the failure will probably occur only once because the damage will likely be irreversible.[12] For these reasons, mutual deterrence is increasingly viewed as a bankrupt policy that we cling to for want of an acceptable alternative.[13]

There is still more. We must realize that deterrence deprives the adversary of a sense of security. After all, one cannot be secure and terrorized at the same time. Therefore, democratic Senator Harkin of Iowa, correctly points out that America cannot improve its security by putting an adversary at risk.[14] What is needed is a common or mutual security. However, deterrence forfeits common security; it is not effective unless overwhelming, and if overwhelming, it creates nuclear instability; that is, in a crisis the adversary is inclined to fire first or have its weapons destroyed.

Actually, two devices nullified the "peace through strength" myth. The first was the hydrogen bomb and the second was the intercontinental ballistic missile. The missiles travel at 15,000 miles per hour and reach their targets in 25 minutes. No nation, no city, and no military target anywhere on the face of the earth is safe from such an attack. The world's largest army cannot repel the arrival and explosion of hydrogen bombs carried in such a missile. A few of those bombs have the capacity to destroy America. After all the money spent on deterrence, arms control, and the preparation for war, America is still defenseless against

such a possibility. It should not be overlooked that a cruise missile lofted over New York from an unmarked ship in a coastal sea lane leaves little to retaliate against.

While our society can be destroyed in an afternoon, and we can fulfill our suicide pact by destroying the other side in half an hour. It is still evident that we are defenseless after spending billions of dollars on defense. It is concluded that deterrence is based on a self-destructive threat that is not credible and can neither prevent war nor an attack on American cities. The threat is simply not believable. Deterrence, as you can see, is a failed policy.

Now it would seem that this knowledge would have ended the matter. The truth is, however, the tilt toward war-fighting continued. In 1984, senior members of the Reagan administration approved the statement of Secretary of Defense Caspar Weinberger, who stated that the U.S. must have the ability to fight and prevail across the full range of plausible nuclear war-fighting scenarios with the Soviet Union.[15] Some statements even became frantic. Paul Nitze, the nuclear statesman declared that even if war were to destroy the world as we know it, the U.S. must win that war decisively.[16] And Mr. Weinberger asserted that the U.S. must not fear war.[17]

More recently a publication on military strategy for the United States speaks of the forces needed to win, and that should deterrence fail, the country must be able to repel or defeat a military attack to end the conflict in a way favorable to the United States.[18] When former Secretary of Defense McNamara referred to the fact that a nuclear war would be the final act in the history of human idiocy, he certainly realized that there would be no favored victor.[19] It is astonishing that the military establishment of the United States is ready, able, and under pressure, willing to plunge the country into the dark abyss of mutual suicide and possibly end life on earth. Today, 30 years later, our policies remain the same as those of the immediate post World War II period.

The situation brings to mind the saying that war is too important to be left to the generals. Sir Winston Churchill's remark that "the Stone Age may return on the gleaming wings of science" has an eloquent chill to it.[20] Yet, the revision of military thinking still awaits in 2000.

♦ ♦ ♦ ♦ ♦

CHAPTER 15 REFERENCES

1. McNamara, R.S. *Blundering into Disaster.* Pantheon Books, New York, 1986, p. 85.
2. Dyer, G. *War.* Crown Publishers, Inc., New York, 1985, p. 207.
3. Ibid., p. 210.
4. Ibid., p. 212.
5. Ibid., p. 213.
6. Callahan, D. *Dangerous Capabilities.* HarperCollins Publishers, New York, 1990, p. 253.
7. Ibid., p. 254.
8. Prins, G. Editor. *The Nuclear Crisis Reader.* Vintage Books, A Division of Random House, New York, 1984, p. 208.
9. Ibid., p. 43.
10. McNamara, R. S. Ibid., p. 114.
11. Prins, G. Ibid., p. 208.
12. Shuman, M. and Sweig, J., Editors. *Conditions of Peace: An Inquiry.* EXPRO Press, Washington, DC, 1991, p. 84.
13. Simon, H.A. "Mutual Deterrence or Nuclear Suicide?" *Science*, Feb. 24, 1984.
14. Harkin, T., and Thomas, C. E. *Five Minutes to Midnight.* A Birch Lane Book, Carol Publishing Group, New York, 1990, p. 121.
15. Prins, G. Ibid., p. 8.
16. Callahan, D. Ibid., p. 165.
17. Prins, G., Ibid., p. 9.
18. Powell, C. L. *The National Military Strategy of the United States,* January 1992, pp. 5, 9.
19. McNamara, R. S. Ibid., p. 144.
20. Prins, G. Ibid., p. 147.

16

History reveals that freedom, justice, and peace always triumph over tyranny and oppression.

The Dominion of Fear

FEAR IS AN EXTREMELY STRONG EMOTION, and it is widely used to control behavior. It molds the attitude of the child who fears a spanking. It tempers the judgment of the criminal who fears incarceration. It encourages religious belief for fear of the unknown. It instills fear in the mind of the addict who avoids apprehension, and it causes fear in the patient who suffers illness. In civil matters, the emotion of fear is useful in similar ways.

Fear also has international effects, especially in the prevention of war. Deterrence depends on threat which is based on using fear. Society, in its desperate attempt to avoid war by threat of retaliation, exploits fear, whereas, secular humanism leans away from fear. It knows that preventing war by preparing for it is a non-sequitur.

Society's exploitation of fear is evidenced by its preparation for war. It turns to the Army, Navy, with its Marine Corps, and Air Force for this purpose. The Army has 500,000 active duty soldiers ready for combat, and 625,000 soldiers in the Army Reserves and National Guard.[1] It operates through use of battle tanks, artillery of various kinds, fighter aircraft, hand arms, gravity bombs, and guided missiles tipped with nuclear warheads.

The firepower of these weapons could destroy civilization.

The U.S. Navy has about 400,000 men and women on active duty, with an additional 170,000 in the Marine Corps.² Their equipment includes aircraft carriers, battleships, cruisers, destroyers, fighter aircraft, and attack and cruise missile submarines. The carriers are the largest warships ever built, with their lengths exceeding three football fields laid end to end. They carry a crew of over 5,000, a complement of over 80 warplanes, and guided missiles with nuclear warheads. Of the 12 aircraft carriers, 7 are nuclear-powered.

Battleships carry the largest guns with a bore of 16 inches that can hurl a shell to a target 20 miles away. Submarines number about 100, some carrying trident nuclear tipped missiles that have a range of about 4,000 miles. Jet fighters and bombers are also part of the force. This armada is divided into two fleets with one for each of the Pacific and Atlantic Oceans.

The U.S. Air Force is the most advanced in the world. It consists of 400,000 active duty troops plus 300,000 in the Air Force Reserve, and 200,000 in civilian roles. It has 6,000 active aircraft divided into hundreds of attack and fighter planes, bombers, transport vessels, and reconnaissance planes. Of special note is the B-2 Stealth plane. The Air Force also has 600 intercontinental ballistic missiles with nuclear warheads. Peacekeeper ICBMs carry 10 nuclear warheads each.³ The planes can out-fly and out-shoot the warplanes of any other nation; and, by refueling in flight, their ranges are extended. There are also helicopter gunships and giant cargo planes to be called on.

Presently over 260,000 troops are stationed overseas, and America maintains a military presence in over 100 countries.⁴ The cost of these preparations for war is astronomical, and overspending is not a recent trend. In 1996, the Defense Monitor reported that the United States continued to spend money it did not have for weapons it did not need, to fight enemies who did not exist.⁵ The military budget for the year 2000 was almost 290 billion dollars, and was projected to exceed 300 billion by 2003.⁶ That would be spending at the rate of a thousand million dollars a day for 300 of the 365 days in the year.

Altogether, it appears that the deterrent capability of the nation is more than enough to prevent war. The enemies that plague us now tend to strike through acts of terrorism, as opposed to outright war. These rogue nations are small and pose little in the way of a striking military threat. The Cold War is over, and the major, even minor, powers are very connected in financial matters, with the economy of each integrated with that of others. Nevertheless, the build-up of weapons continues. It is beyond what is needed, and is due to an excess of fear.

The attitude about this from the average citizen is that they'd rather have too much than too little, expressing the fear of insufficient arms. The politician has three reasons to be fearful, and they are related to winning elections, not to weapons. The first is to avoid being labeled soft on defense, which is political suicide. The second is to avoid base closings in his/her own jurisdiction; and, the third is to guarantee that no foreign nation will attack.⁷ The public is comforted by the congressional official who protects the nation; expense be damned. Fear continues to exert its effect.

Examples of over-arming are astonishing. The Pentagon now recommends a fleet of three new-type warplanes to replace the present force. One of the new planes, of which hundreds will be needed, costs 190 million dollars. About this, it is reported that what makes this plan so questionable is the undeniable fact that the United States can maintain total global air supremacy well into the 21st Century with its present fleet of more than 3,800 unmatched Navy, Marine, and Air Force tactical fighter/attack aircraft.⁸ The Pentagon's program for new planes is projected to cost a total of 350 billion dollars, making it the most expensive military program in history. About this, George Kennan, Dean of American Diplomats, has said that the annual spending of hundreds of billions of dollars on defense has developed into a national addiction.[9]

Some years ago the Pentagon undertook a Bottom-up-Review in which it recommended the capability of fighting two wars at once and without the help of allies. The wars were referred to as Major Regional Conflicts, or MRCs. This occasioned an enormous additional expense. Subsequently, then Secretary of Defense William Perry, in testimony before Congress, stated that because it was nowhere in the planning, he believed it was an implausible scenario that the U.S. would ever have to fight two wars at the same time.[10] Nevertheless, a subsequent Quadrenial Defense Review (QDR), which examined the matter, left intact the 2MRC requirement. With tongue in cheek, it could be pointed out that a third separate army would give the United States even more security.

Retired U.S. Senator Dale Bumpers has become the Director of the Center for Defense Information with headquarters in Washington, DC. In a letter he points out that President Clinton recommended a 12 billion dollar increase in the military budget for Fiscal Year (FY) 2000. To this the Congress gratuitously added 8 billion. Director Bumpers then declared that this is the way Congress proves it's tougher on defense than the President. That is his interpretation. The 8 billion also expresses the fear of Congress that its investment in deterrence is inadequate. It is a fear-driven idea that after a certain level is reached, more weapons equate with more security. Moreover, hiding behind weapons is neither courageous nor brave. Nor is it wise. More weapons to prepare for World War III will not make Americans more secure.

Another expression of fear is the fortification of American embassies abroad. In recent months two have been bombed, one in Nairobi, and the other in Dar es Salaam. More recently, crowds have burned U.S. flags and stoned U.N. offices in Pakistan.[11] Out of fear that such events will be repeated, the Clinton administration has increased its FY 2000 budget request for embassy construction from 36 million to 300 million.[12] The cry is to build bunker-like chanceries designed to be blast-proof, and impenetrable. Can such buildings properly represent democracy? Hardly. Would they thwart terrorists? Only somewhat. Would they strengthen America's role? No.[13]

The last example of fear on the international scene is failure of the Congress to ratify the Comprehensive Test Ban Treaty (CTBT). Banning of nuclear weapons began in 1991 when the first Strategic Arms Reduction Treaty (START I) was signed by Presidents Bush and Yeltsin. In 1993 a START II agreement calling for further reductions of strategic nuclear weapons to levels between 3,000 and 3,500 for each side was signed by the two presidents. However, the U.S. Senate did not ratify this treaty until 1996, and Russia has still not ratified it. The existence of thousands of nuclear weapons ten years after the fall of the Berlin Wall is startling and dangerous. A single warhead is capable of destroying an entire city by incinerating hundreds of square miles. Thus, as Miller points out, the Cold War is still not over.[14]

In 1999, President Clinton asked Congress to ratify the Comprehensive Test Ban Treaty (CTBT) which would prohibit testing of our strategic nuclear weapons now in storage and aging. The treaty has already been ratified by many of our allies. Congress failed to ratify for fear other nations, potential adversaries, could possibly surpass us in weapon developments. Even the Chairman of the Armed Services Committee, Senator John Warner, refused to ratify. There were still the political fears (soft on defense, loss of bases), and the possibility of foreign military superiority. After reviewing the matter, Hans Bethe, Nobel Laureate in Physics and former member of the President's

Science Advisory Committee, refuted these fears, and declared that the vote against the test ban treaty undermined the entire future of arms control.[15] While the treaty may eventually be ratified, it is evident that the dominion of fear is extremely broad.

In confronting these matters, Secular Humanism would likely have been guided more by reason than by fear. It would probably not have yielded to the phantom scare of fighting two wars at once. It would have saved for domestic use the billions unnecessarily spent on sophisticated aircraft; and, it would certainly have transferred to next year's budget the 8 billion dollar gift to the President from the Congress. Also, it would have reconsidered the role of the embassies rather than fortifying them in hostile territory, and it would have worked harder to ratify the Comprehensive Test Ban Treaty. These would have been significant improvements over the conditions that now prevail.

One of the main improvements would have been a re-allo-

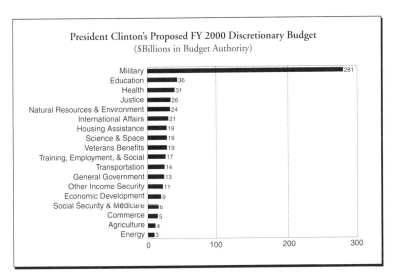

Fig. J. Disparity between civilian and military spending for 1999.

cation of military funds to the civilian needs of the nation. This is shown in Figure J which reveals the disparity between military and civilian spending.[16] Without this re-allocation civil programs will have to be markedly reduced in order to provide for the military expense without exceeding the national budget.

The greatest improvement that Secular Humanism could make would be to turn away from confrontation with other countries and toward cooperation with them. In 1994, President Clinton declared in the preface to his National Security Strategy speech that American leadership in the world has never been more essential.[17] America thus empowered itself to intervene militarily any place in the world against whatever it considered against its best interests. This option then broadened into a moral right to dictate decisions and control events wherever they run counter to the wishes of the government. In this way, America becomes, at high cost, policeman to the world. However, it is doubtful that military power can shape the world and create empires without destroying the world in the process. That would, of course, be an unspeakable result of policy. It is perhaps time for a great turning.

One turn is downward to the low road. It relies on confrontation, military force, deterrence, threat, fear, and ill will. It seeks to dominate, and, under the name of leadership, to control events not sanguine to our own needs. Superior weapons, confrontation, and international control are the tactics of the bully. They do not build amicable relationships. They are self-seeking by threat of force. They depend on retaliation, and they prepare for war. The low road is based on fear, it cannot avoid ill will, and it is isolating, desultory, and morally in doubt, making it unworthy of a great nation.

The turn upward is to the high road. It relies on international cooperation. It thrives on foreign aid and economic development. It shares and helps. It de-emphasizes militarism by not trumpeting its superior weapons or broadcasting its overwhelming military force. It does not speak of war. It leads by helping others. It shuns fear and threat. It lives on goodwill, and it is the tactic of peace. It is the strategy of which the nation can be proud.

Will the nation be guided by the dominion of fear and take the low road with ill will, threat, moral question, and the risk of war, or will it take the high road that is morally sound, and trust in goodwill, sharing, and economic development? In the age of hydrogen bombs, that is an especially poignant question. It is the very type that one would think religious leaders would address constantly since it is a great moral issue. It is a question that Secular Humanists do not back away from, as the movement is based on fact.

♦ ♦ ♦ ♦ ♦

CHAPTER 16 REFERENCES

1. "Army." *World Book Encyclopedia.* 1: 726, 1999.
2. "Navy." *World Book Encyclopedia.* 14: 76, 1999.
3. "Air Force." *World Book Encyclopedia.* 1: 182, 1999.
4. Brembeck, H.S., and Cortright, D. "A Better Policy For a Safer World." *Inforum,* No. 25, Autumn, 1999.
5. "The New Military Budget: Unlimited Ambition, Limited Money." *The Defense Monitor* 25, No.3, 1996, p. 5.
6. "The Fiscal Year 1999 Military Budget." Ibid., 27, No. 4, 1998, p. 1.
7. "Military Domination or Constructive Leadership?" Ibid., 27, No. 3, 1998, p. 2.
8. "Do We Really Need Three Fighters?" Ibid., 28, No. 2, 1999, P. 1.
9. "Hegemony Asserts the Dean of Our Diplomats." Ibid., 27, No. 3, 1998, p. 4.
10. "Top Seven Claims Why We Need to Increase Military Spending." Ibid., No. 4, 1998, p. 4.
11. "Crowds burn U.S. Flags and Stone U.N. Offices." *News-Press.* Ft. Myers, FL. Nov. 11, 1999.
12. Loeffler, J. C. "Embassies Under Siege: They Deserve Better." *G.W. Magazine,* Fall, 1999, p. 1.
13. Ibid., p. 1.
14. Millar, A. "The Cold War is (Not) Over." *Inforum,* No. 25, Autumn, 1999.
15. Bethe, H. A. "The Treaty Betrayed." *The New York Review,* Oct. 21, 1999.
16. "The Fiscal Year 2000 Military Budget." *The Defense Monitor,* 28, No. 1, 1999, p. 1.
17. "Military Domination or Constructive Leadership?" *The Defense Monitor,* 27, No. 3, 1998, p. 1.

Conclusion

The main conclusion of this set of essays is that there is no reason to suppose a deity exists; and, if there is no deity, it is likely that Christ was not divine; and, we are probably alone on the crust of this minor planet. There are those who would pale at this conclusion. It is one of magnitude, but the reasoning is indisputable. We have to step forward and acknowledge that. We have to accept this conclusion that appears to have a crushing effect on established religions, and especially on Christianity.

In a dynamic world things are bound to change. The mechanism of change is either objective evidence or irrefutable reason. The conclusion of these essays can be looked on as change of the latter type. It is radical and disturbing, but it is beneficial in the long run because it complies with the facts and leaves us free from the fear of acknowledging the truth.

To capsulate the focus of these essays, it was put forth that postulates without evidence are meaningless; that Christian morals are valid while Christian myths are not; that only objective evidence is reliable; that the church and state must be kept separate; and, that vengeance should be expunged from the treatment of crime.

It was also pointed out that nonviolence is the superior response to violence; that the Bible is not always correct; that the clergy are not endowed with special knowledge or authority in the abortion matter; and, that the sacrifice of women in order to protect fetuses is morally in doubt. Therefore, it could be agreed that these conditions are more closely approximated by Secular Humanism than by conventional Christianity or other religions.

Lastly, without help from elsewhere, we humans will have to contend with our own problems and manage them. It should be said that there is something exciting and gratifying about this. To know that it is up to no one but ourselves to face the problems we contend with daily is somehow stimulating. If it can be done, it is up to us alone. And it can be done, even if our lives have to be given up to accomplish it. We have not marched through four thousand million years of evolution to be defeated now. So we should take heart; we must take heart. It is all before us, and our ingenuity, our faith in each other, and our spirit of goodwill will bring us through.

Nevertheless, it won't be easy. The great river of life flows on, slowly, inexorably, and blindly. It has no mind; its destiny is not predetermined. It is unfeeling, and it knows neither guilt nor remorse. The mighty river is evolution, and it is unavoidable. The field and the meadow and the mountain may appear serene, but within species an ongoing war exists between the able and those less so.

The war also goes on between species: The ant eats the aphid; the bat swallows the insect; the otter eats the clam; the grizzly rips the flesh of the jumping salmon, the orca crushes the bones of the living seal; the hawk flies off with the struggling meerkat; the eagle sinks its talons into the flesh of the dozing fish; wild dogs rip the belly of the running antelope; the crocodile drowns the thrashing wildebeest; the buffalo gores the lion; the lion throttles the zebra; and, the lurking hyena dismembers the injured gazelle. Animals seldom die quiet deaths; they are often eaten alive. The struggle to eat or be eaten is universal. Even humans, in the exigency of war, kill millions of their own kind. Thus the river of life runs on in savage turmoil. Only morality, born in the mind of man, tempers the rawness of the flow.

How should mankind proceed so as to ensure security and equanimity? Four general rules will help. First, the truth must be proclaimed wherever it is found. Second, illusion must be unveiled whenever it is seen. Third, hate must be dissipated wherever it occurs. Fourth, enlargement of the hearts and minds of all people must be encouraged. This, without a doubt, is the way forward.

✦ ✦ ✦ ✦ ✦

You may order
And Man Created God... by Chandler Smith
ISBN 1-56550-086-5
from your local bookstore, Amazon.com, or
directly from the publisher.

To order copies directly from VBI by mail use this order form:

Number of books:_____at $10.00 per book $_____

Sales tax of 7.25% applies to books mailed to California addresses only:

Number of books:_____ at $0.73 per copy $_____

Shipping and handling at $3.50 for first book
(add $2 for each additional book) _____books $_____

                      Total amount enclosed $_____

Name:_____

Mailing address:_____

City:_____State:_____Zip_____

Please send a check or money order (no cash or C.O.D.) to:
Vision Books International
775 East Blithedale Ave. #342
Mill Valley, CA 94941

Visit our Web site at www.vbipublishing.com